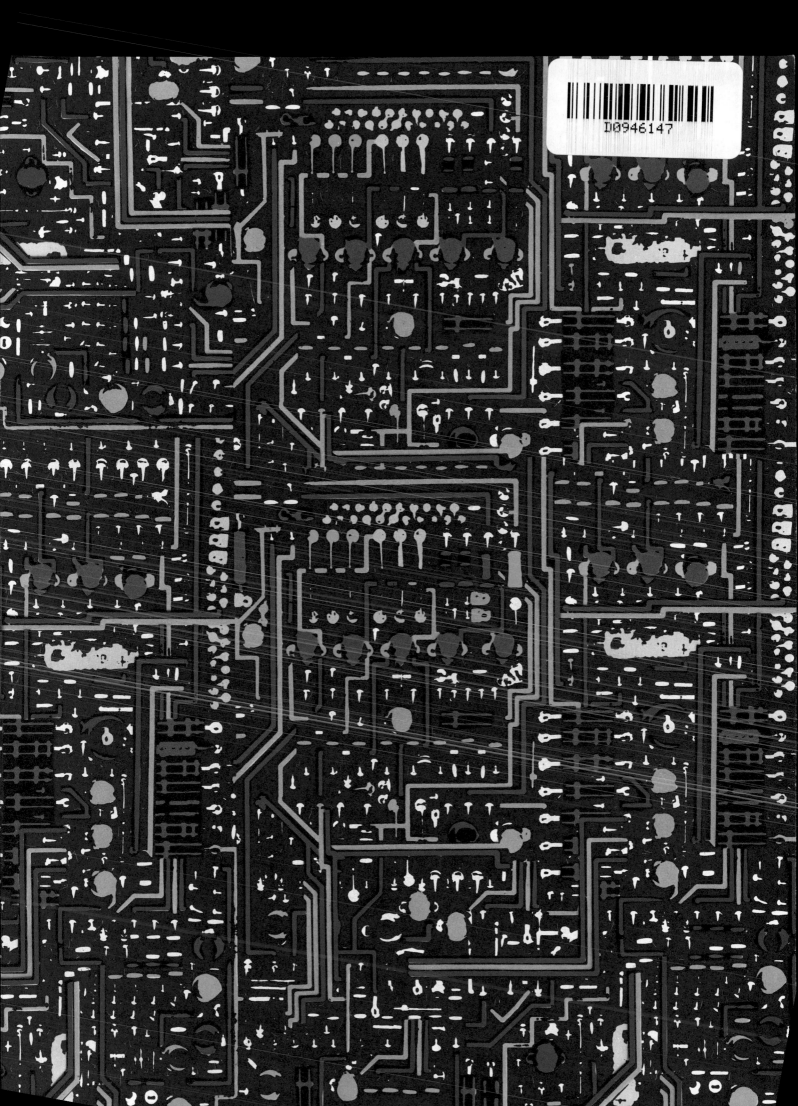

THE ROBOT BOOK

BY ROBERT MALONE

EDITOR
WILLIAM E. MALONEY

PRODUCER
JEAN-CLAUDE SUARÈS

DESIGN DIRECTOR
SEYMOUR CHWAST

DESIGNER
RICHARD MANTEL

Created and Produced by
Push Pin Press
A Harvest/HBJ Book

A PUSH PIN PRESS BOOK

Producer: Jean-Claude Suares
Editorial Director: William E. Maloney
Design Director: Seymour Chwast

Printed in the United States of America

Library of Congress Catalog Card Number
77-92555

ISBN 0-15-678452-1

First Harvest/HBJ edition 1978

A B C D E

JOVE PUBLICATIONS, INC.
(Harcourt Brace Jovanovich)
757 Third Avenue, New York, N.Y. 10017

You may picture robots as large, mechanical men with laser eyes, who clank when they walk, threaten civilization, and seem abnormally interested in blondes, sometimes carrying them off to wherever robots carry blondes off to.

Or maybe you see robots as docile machines, toiling away for their human masters, untiring, uncomplaining, doing the dull jobs humans don't want to do.

Or if you have seen *Star Wars*, you may picture robots as friendly machines that have been programmed to upstage human actors, getting star billing and the best laughs in the movie. Robots are all of these, but much, much more.

There are robots in fiction, smarter than humans. Also robots in fiction too dumb to come out of the rain (so that they rust and end up on the junk pile). There are robots (called automatons) that look human, can play chess, draw pictures, and give piano concerts. There are industrial robots that do work humans once did, but have no resemblance to humans at all. There are robot devices that wash our clothes, cook our food, turn on the heat or air conditioning, and take on jobs in space and in medicine.

The robot fascinates man because it is the machine that most resembles man himself. "Why it's almost human," spectators say with awe when they see the robot figure of Lincoln rise from his chair at Disney World in Florida, then deliver the Gettysburg Address. An industrial robot at work on an automobile assembly line may start you wondering if human workers are necessary at all.

With advances in science and technology, humans will be creating "smarter" robots. These robots will be doing more and more things that humans now do. We may begin to feel that they are intruding in almost every aspect of our lives.

It's time we start finding out what robots are all about.

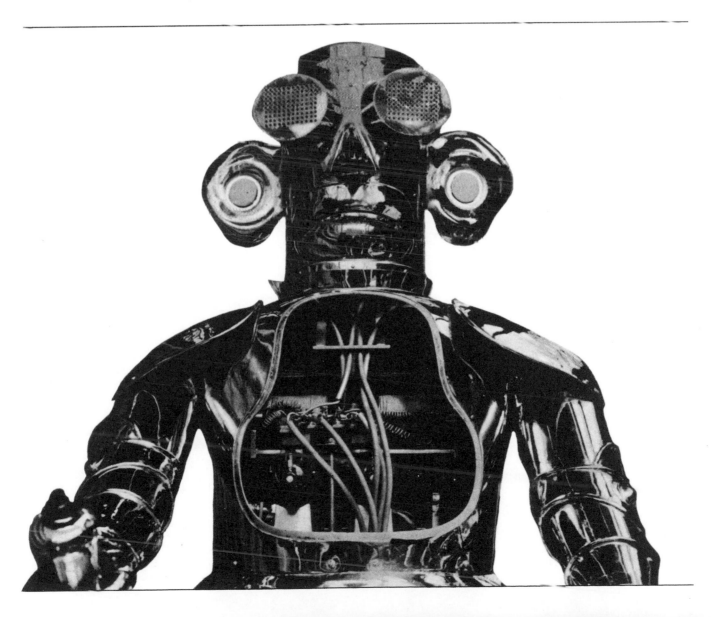

CONTENTS

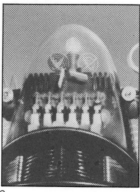

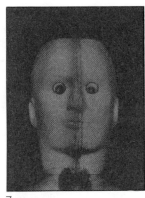

CHRONOLOGY OF ROBOT-RELATED EVENTS

3000 B.C. Egyptian tools, mass labor, water clocks, articulated figures, and oracles

2000–500 Egyptian and Greek astronomical models

350 Euclid's geometry, Greece

100 Hero of Alexandria's automatons and automatic steam-driven machines

50 Concept of atomic structure by Titus Lucretius, Rome

100 B.C., concept by Hero of Alexandria

1044 A.D. Movable type by Pi Sheng, China

1050 Workable lenses by Alhazen, Persia

1105 Windmill in France

1160 Magnetic compass in China

1180 Fixed steering rudder, Europe

1298 Spinning wheel, introduced in Europe, from India

1300 Horizontal windmill by Al-Dimashqi, Persia

1315 Automated devices by Al-Jazari, Persia

1315 Medical dissection of the human body by Raimondo de Luzzi, Italy

1345 Division of hours and minutes into sixties, Europe

1350 Automatic cock figure for Strasbourg cathedral, Germany

1370 Metal type in Korea

1420 Velocipede by Fontana, Italy

1438 Wind turbine by Mariano, Italy

1450 Printing press by Johann Gutenberg, Germany

1472–1519 Concepts for centrifugal pump, universal joint, conical screw, belt drive, link chains, bevel, and spiral gears by Leonardo da Vinci, Italy

1500 Portable watch by Peter Henlein, Germany

1558 Camera lens and stop elements by Daniello Barbaro, Italy

1579 Automatic ribbon machine in Danzig, Poland

1580 Golem concept by Rabbi Judah Low, Prague

1608 Telescope by Hans Lippersheim, Holland

1609 Laws of motion by Galileo Galilei, Italy

1614 Logarithms by John Napier, England

1620 Primitive adding machine by John Napier, England

1628 Circulation of the blood by William Harvey, England

1630 Steam engine by David Ramsey, Scotland

1642 Desk-top calculator by Blaise Pascal, France

1650 Magic lantern by Athanasius Kircher, Italy

1652 Air pump by Otto von Guericke, Germany

1658 Balance springs for clocks by Robert Hooke, England

1671 Speaking tube by Morland, England

1672 First electrical machine by Otto von Guericke, Germany

1673 Improved calculator by Gottfried von Leibniz, Germany

1682 Law of gravitation by Isaac Newton, England

1687 *Principia* by Isaac Newton, England

1711 Sewing Machine by De Camus, France

1714 Typewriter concept by Henry Mill, England

1727 Light images using silver nitrate by Johann Heinrich Schulze, Germany

1730 Jacques de Vaucanson's duck automatons and assorted android figures, France

1745 Leyden jar, an early electrical condenser, Holland

1750 Pierre and Henri-Louis Jacquet-Droz's automaton, Switzerland

1721-1790, Pierre Jaquet-Droz, automaton-maker

1761 Air cylinders by Smeaton, England

1767 Spinning jenny by James Hargreaves, England

1769 Automaton chess player by Wolfgang von Kempelen, Germany

1785 Interchangeable parts by Le Blanc, France

1785 Power loom by Edmund Cartwright, England

1791 Discovery of animal electricity by Luigi Galvani, Italy

1793 Cotton gin by Eli Whitney, U.S.

1797 Screw-cutting lathe by Henry Maudslay, England

1800 Galvanic cell by Alessandro Volta, Italy

1804 Loom using punched cards by Joseph Jacquard, France

1815 Automatic draughtsman by Henri Maillardet, Switzerland

1817 Discovery of feedback and control in animal systems by François Magendie, France

1817 *Frankenstein* by Mary Shelley, England

1822 Electric motor by Michael Faraday, England

1823 "Difference engine" for calculating by Charles Babbage, England

1831 Inductive electricity by Michael Faraday, England

1833 Analytical engine by Charles Babbage, England

1838 Electromagnetic telegraph by Samuel Morse, U.S.

1839 Vulcanization of rubber by Charles Goodyear, U.S.

1926, the robot Maria from Fritz Lang's film Metropolis

1839 Daguerreotype by Louis Daguerre, France

1841 Paper positives in photography by William Talbot, England

1848 Study of nerve impulses in frogs by Hermann Helmholtz, Germany

1851 Crystal Palace exhibit in London, England

1854 *An Investigation of the Laws of Thought* by George Boole, England

1855 Concept of television transmission by Caselle

1856 Modern steel by Henry Bessemer, England

1864 Primitive motion picture device by Ducos de Havron, France

1865 Genetics by Gregor Mendel, Austria

1868 *The Theory of Governors* by James Maxwell, England

1870 Celluloid by John Hyatt, England

1872 Automatic air brakes by George Westinghouse, U.S.

1872 *Erewhon* by Samuel Butler, England

1875 Recording of animal brain waves by Fritsch and Hitzig, Germany

1876 Beam engine with governor at Philadelphia Exposition, U.S.

1876 Electric telephone by Alexander Graham Bell, U.S.

1877 Microphone by Thomas Edison, U.S.

1877 Phonograph by Thomas Edison, U.S.

1879 Carbon lamp by Thomas Edison, U.S.

1887 Integrated telephone system by Alexander Graham Bell, U.S.

1888 Recording adding machine by William S. Burroughs, U.S.

1890 Beginning of data processing, punch card machines by Herman Hollerith, U.S.

1894 Talking doll by Thomas Edison, U.S.

1895 Motion picture projector by

Thomas Edison, U.S.

1895 Radiotelegraphy by Guglielmo Marconi, Italy

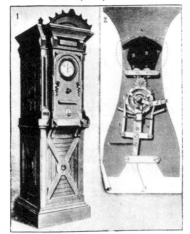

1895, *French automatic vending machine*

1898 *The War of the Worlds* by H. G. Wells, England

1903 Electrocardiograph by Willem Einthoven, Holland

1903 "Round Trip to the Year 2000" by William Wallace Cook, U.S.

1906 Vacuum tube by Lee De Forest, U.S.

1909 *Moxon's Master* by Ambrose Bierce, U.S.

1910 Gyro compass by Elmer Sperry, U.S.

1911 *Ralph 124C41 +* by Hugo Gernsback, birth of modern science fiction, U.S.

1912 *The Machine Stops* by E. M. Forster, England

1914 Modern chess-playing machine by Torres y Quevedo, Spain

1916 *The Golem* by Gustav Meyrirk, Prague

1921 *R.U.R.* by Karel Capek, birth of word *robot*, Prague

1926 *Metropolis* by Fritz Lang, Germany

1927 Television by Philo Farnsworth, U.S.

1927 Differential analyzer, a working electronic computer, by Vannevar Bush, U.S.

1929 Electroencephalograph by Hans Berger, Germany

1930–40 Robot stories by Eando Binder, U.S.

1932 Homeostasis concept described by W. B. Cannon, England

1932 Alpha robot at London Fair, England

1935, *illustration by Marchioni for* Astounding Stories

1938 Information theory by Claude Shannon, U.S.

1939 Electro robot by Westinghouse at New York World's Fair, U.S.

1942–49 Foundation series and Three laws of Robotics by Isaac Asimov, U.S.

1944 ENIAC, first digital computer by J. Presper Eckert and John W. Mauchly, U.S.

1948 Transistor by John Bardeen, Walter Brattain, and William Shockley, U.S.

1948 Cybernetic Theory by Norbert Wiener, U.S.

1948 Homeostat by W. R. Ashby, ran on negative feedback, England

1949 *A Mathematical Theory of Communication* by Claude Shannon and Warren Weaver, U.S.

1950 Industrial robot research and development by Unimation, U.S.

1954 Maser by Charles Townes, U.S.

1958 First implantable pacemaker by Earl Bakken, U.S.

1964 IBM computer system 360 introduced, U.S.

1965 *The Cyberiad* by Stanislaw Lem, U.S.

1967 *2001, A Space Odyssey,* by Arthur Clarke, film by Stanley Kubrick, U.S.–England

1967 Human heart transplant by Christiaan Barnard, South Africa

1970 Space probes using robot explorers, U.S.

1972 Robot in *Silent Running,* Douglas Trumbell, director, U.S.

1977 C-3PO and R2-D2 robots in *Star Wars* by George Lucas, U.S.

1978 Robot machines at work throughout industry, U.S., Europe, Japan

1976, *robot lander searches for life on Mars*

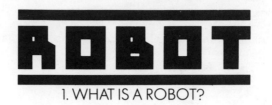

ROBOT

1. WHAT IS A ROBOT?

The word *robot* was coined in 1921 by Karel Capek, a Czech dramatist, for his play *R.U.R.* (Rossum's Universal Robots). In Capek's nightmare vision, the robots were invented to save humans from having to work, but they developed a distaste for imperfect and frail humanity and took over the world. If not downright evil, they were certainly sinister creatures whose values had nothing to do with man's. Contrary to the purpose for which they had been created, they tore down what humans had taken centuries to build, and in the end destroyed mankind itself.

Machines were becoming uncomfortably sophisticated and "smart." As a symbol of the uneasy side of relations between man and machine, robots caught on immediately. Although the play itself was a mediocre one, it enjoyed successful productions in London and New York due to the strength of its central idea. A host of imitators filled books and magazines with similar tales. Soon the word *robot* came to stand for any machine that replaced a human.

What scared people about the robots was their intelligence. Intelligence had always been the difference between men and animals, and men and machines. The existence of smart machines raised the question: just what is it that makes human beings better than other creatures?

Robots hit us where we were most embarrassingly imperfect. They did not tire, nor did they complain. There wasn't an irrational bolt in their bodies.

Since those days, we have come to be familiar with real robots. They regulate our traffic, fly our airplanes, guide our ships, step in where conditions would be too perilous for us. They do calculations for us that would take us years to do on paper. But they do not take over.

Above: Henri Maillardet made this automaton in 1811. She could write and draw pictures. Her insides were a complicated arrangement of clockwork and mechanical linkages. She was designed to be as human, in as many details of her dress, features, and movements, as was possible.

Opposite: A century later, clockwork gave way to electricity, and human features to the features of the man-machine. This robot was displayed in London in 1928. The initials on his chest, R.U.R., are to remind us of Karel Capek's play.

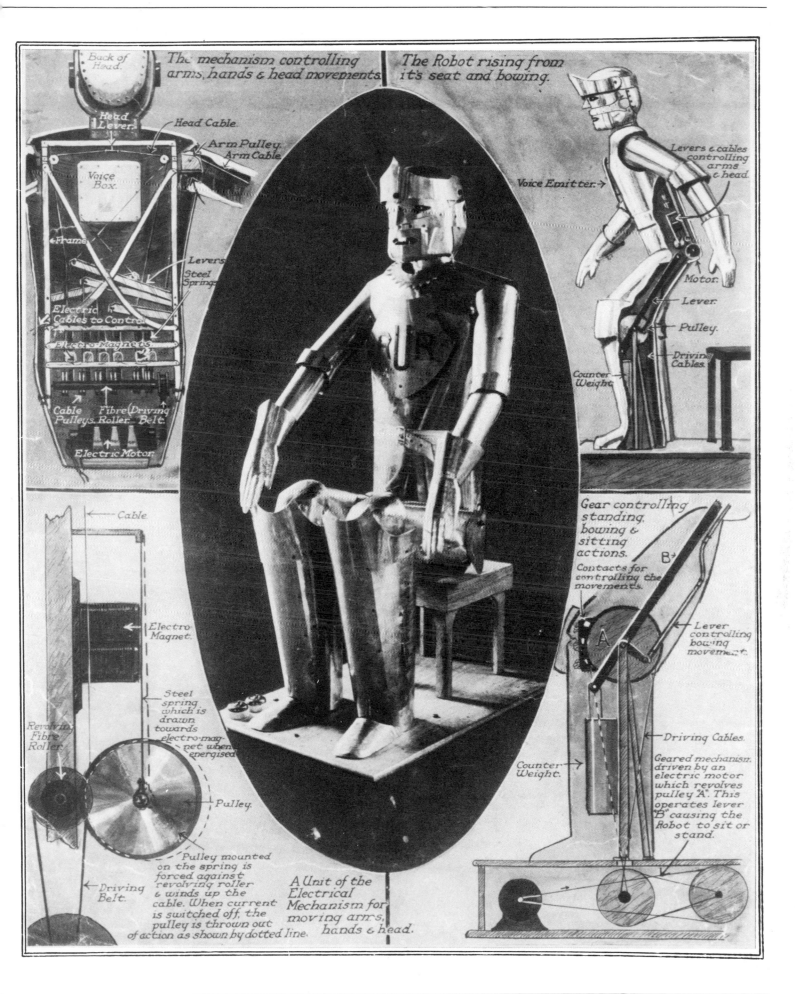

The mechanism controlling arms, hands & head movements.

The Robot rising from it's seat and bowing.

Back of Head.

Head Lever.

Head Cable.

Arm Pulley.
Arm Cable

Voice Box.

Frame

Levers.

Steel Springs.

Electric Cables to Control

Electro-Magnets

Cable Pulleys.

Fibre Driving Roller.

Belt.

Electric Motor.

Levers & cables controlling arms & head.

Voice Emitter. →

Motor.

Lever.

Pulley.

Driving Cables.

Counter Weight.

Cable

Electro Magnet.

Steel spring which is drawn towards electro-magnet when energised.

Revolving Fibre Roller.

Pulley.

Pulley mounted on the spring is forced against revolving roller & winds up the cable. When current is switched off, the pulley is thrown out of action as shown by dotted line.

Driving Belt.

A Unit of the Electrical Mechanism for moving arms, hands & head.

Gear controlling standing, bowing & sitting actions.

Contacts for controlling the movements.

B

A

Lever controlling bowing movement.

Driving Cables.

Geared mechanism driven by an electric motor which revolves pulley "A". This operates lever "B" causing the Robot to sit or stand.

Counter Weight.

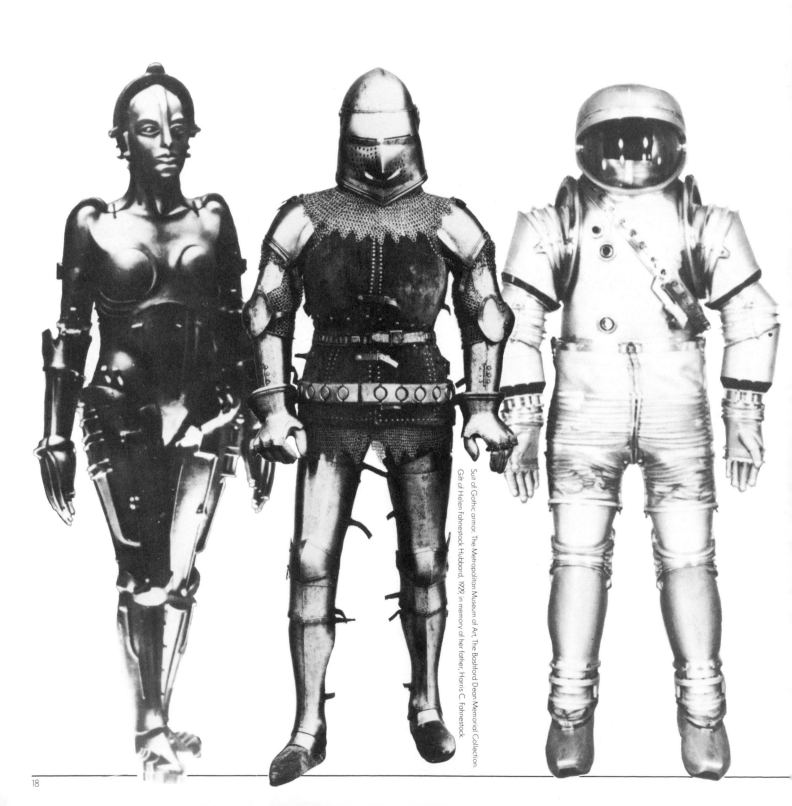

Suit of Gothic armor. The Metropolitan Museum of Art, The Bashford Dean Memorial Collection. Gift of Helen Fahnestock Hubbard, 1929, in memory of her father, Harris C. Fahnestock.

Opposite, left: The robot Maria, from Fritz Lang's 1926 film *Metropolis,* set the style early on for machines whose symbolic humanity outweighed their mechanical origins. She is, quite clearly, the evil grandmother of the 1977 robot C-3PO of *Star Wars.*

Opposite, middle: As early as 1400, armor makers had solved the problems of articulation. What lay ahead of them was the difficult job of filling up the insides with machinery.

Opposite, right: The same solutions to the problem of articulation were applied in NASA's 1964 prototype for a space suit to be used for the 1969 moon landing. It turned out to be clumsy. What was suitable for a purely schematic and theoretical mechanical man proved cumbersome for flesh and blood.

Right: Robby, from the film *The Invisible Boy,* is clearly the symbol of a rather benign technology. His shape has no functional relationship to the way he operates. He is just fun to look at. The people the film was made for did not care that there was an actor inside him.

Right: By contrast, Sherwin H. Feuhrer's robot, which won a prize at the 1955 Ford Industrial Arts Show, was a pure machine. Nonetheless, its appeal depended a lot on its resemblance to the shape of the human body.

From the MGM release Forbidden Planet © 1956 by Metro-Goldwyn-Mayer, Inc.

Right: The movie wasn't much, nor was the robot. By the time this film was made, all the moviegoers needed was the skimpiest collection of hardware, your basic tin woodsman; they supplied the rest.

Below: Real robots tend not to look like humans at all. The Lear Siegler Mailmobile can navigate a course through an office at a speed of one mile an hour. It is programmed to stop at stations along its route. Although it weighs 700 pounds and can carry up to 500 pounds of mail, memos, and packages, it will stop immediately on contact with any obstacle. It announces its arrival with flashing blue lights and a soft beeping tone. A model of mechanical discretion, it does not try to date the secretaries.

Opposite: When functional robots do have eyes, ears, or hands, these organs do not tend to look like their human counterparts. The Mobot Mark II, designed by the Hughes Aircraft Company to replace humans in dangerous environments, can be operated by remote control. Its television camera eyes permit it to "see" from two angles simultaneously. Its hands can pick up delicate objects safely. The Mobot can collect and transmit data, but there still has to be a human being on the other end to figure out what it all means.

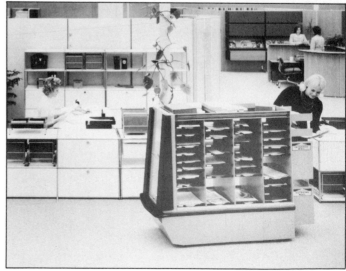

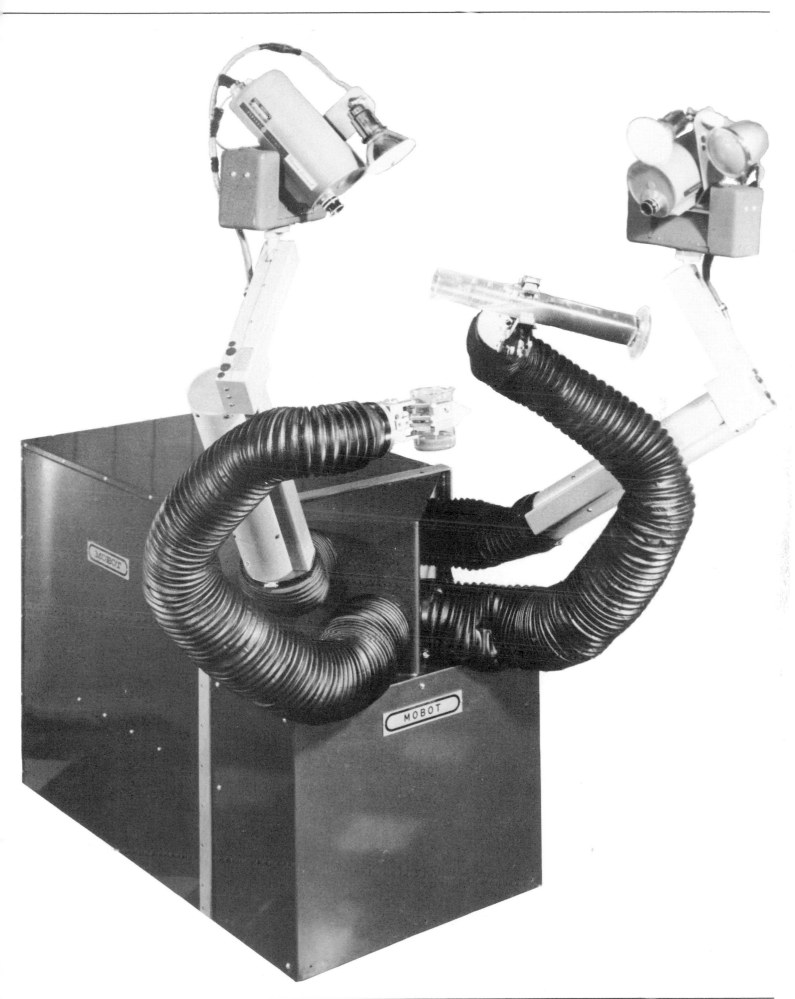

ROBOT

2. ORIGINS

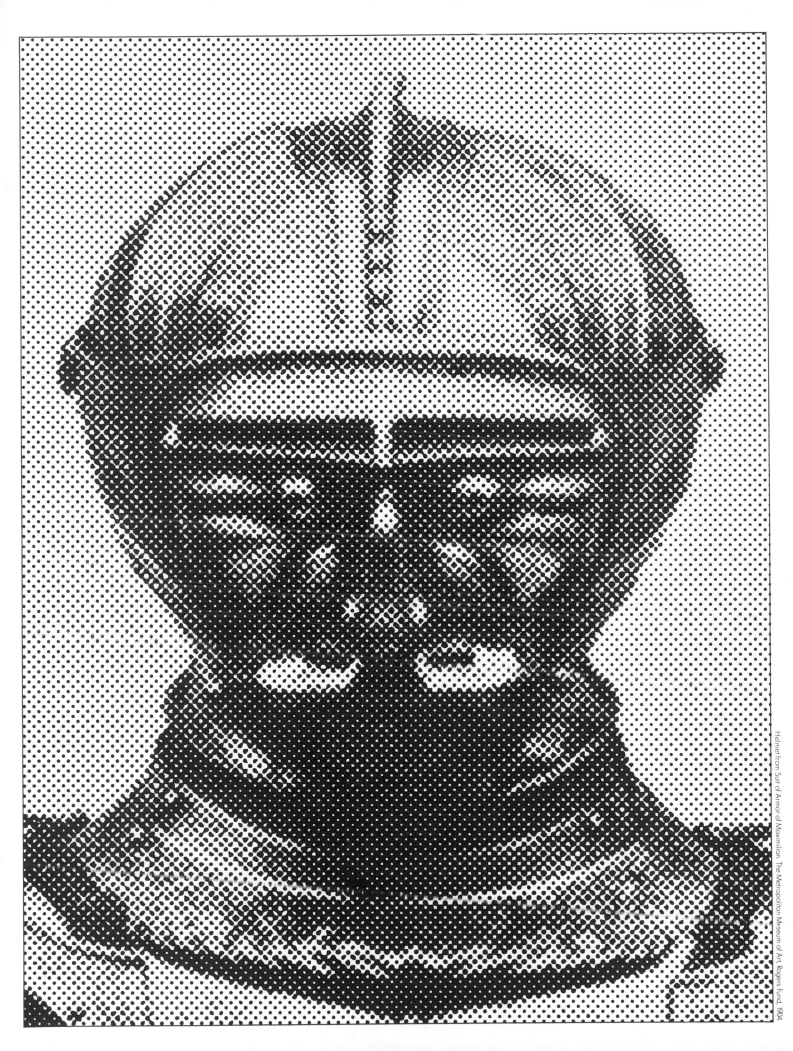

The earliest ancestors of the robots were simple creations, crude in concept and in execution. They seem hardly recognizable to us as machines that imitated life. We have lost our sense of wonder, accustomed as we are to machines that perform every conceivable function, and even turn themselves on and off.

Primitive people believed that gods inhabited the wind and the seas and that trees contained the captured spirits of living beings. They worshiped the animals whose attributes they admired or needed most. For them, motion was a proof of life. To be able to make a moving, therefore living, imitation of a creature was to be able to control that creature. No wonder the first automatons were the property of the shamans.

Technology is the enemy of magic, and it is easy to see why. For a long time primitive man was able to make a doll out of mud and pretend it moved, or make people believe it moved. In order to make an automaton—to make a doll that really moved, the person who made it had to understand at least the most basic rudiments of mechanics. This was a great first step in the direction of technology.

Opposite: The god that speaks to man: concealed behind this mask of the jackal god Anubis, the priests of ancient Egypt issued their pronouncements. Behind the moving jaw, there is a speaking trumpet. The Wizard of Oz resorted to similar, if more sophisticated, devices until he was unmasked by Toto.

Below: This graceful sculpted dog was found in an Egyptian tomb dating about 2000 B.C. When a lever in the stomach is moved, the dog's mouth opens. The figure is modeled after the Saluki, an ancient hunting breed. The dog was probably placed in the tomb to serve his master in the afterlife.

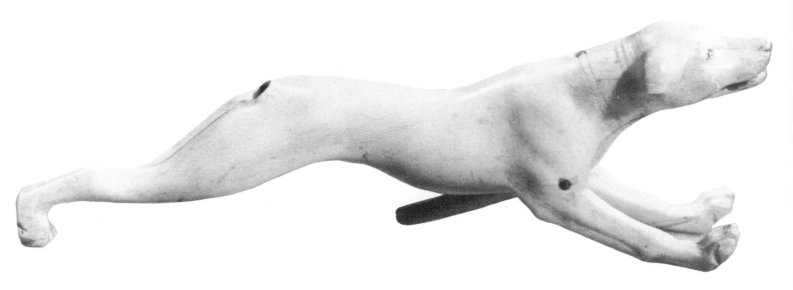

Hound in full cry. Egyptian. Ivory. The Metropolitan Museum of Art, Rogers Fund, 1940.

To the people of early cultures, dolls, puppets, and other articulated figures seemed to have a life of their own. To be able to reproduce a characteristic movement was a great triumph. Using pins, strings, and any other mechanisms to produce movement, they celebrated their understanding of the world around them.

What they could not create themselves, they had the gods create, monsters and hybrids of all kinds, terrible and powerful. Hephaestus created Talos, a bronze giant who could be killed only by removing a pin from his heel to let his vital fluid run out. These creations all shared certain things: they were more powerful than humans, they represented obstacles to a human achieving something he wanted, and they could be overcome by human ingenuity.

In classical Greece, the idea of the functional robot was born. In the fourth century B.C., Aristotle wrote: "If every instrument could accomplish its own work, obeying or anticipating the will of others…if the shuttle could weave, and the pick touch the lyre, without a hand to guide them, chief workmen would not need servants, nor masters slaves."

Aristotle was describing the very essence of technology—to make the loom itself the weaver, the instrument the player; he was describing automation. It took centuries before that vision began to be possible, but the seed was already sown.

Musée National du Louvre/Antiquités Égyptiennes

Above: Man got the first clues about the way mechanics work by examining the way the joints of living creatures moved. This painted wooden baker from ancient Egypt pounds grain with the stone held in his hands. Crude as it is, the doll shows that the person who made it understood how axles, levers, and fulcrums and even counterweights worked.

Opposite: The Eskimo people of southwestern Alaska used articulated masks in rituals that portrayed the movements of the sun and moon. The Indian people of the northwest created similar masks, which usually have four arms that open and close, controlled by strings. This ritualistic creation of the cosmos led eventually to the creation of calendars, astrolabes, sundials, and water clocks. These devices were among the first complex machines made by man.

Eskimo mask. Milwaukee Public Museum.

Although their leisure time was based on slave labor, the Egyptians, and later the Greeks, spent a lot of it thinking about machines.

They had already figured out that it was not magic that made the universe work. Aristotle, Euclid, Archimedes, and others had made astronomical, physical, and mathematical calculations with a high degree of accuracy. They were able to apply some of this science to everyday life. They discovered that the ramp, lever, sledge, pulley, wheel, and cylinder could be used to overcome the effects of gravity and friction; in other words, these devices could be used to do man's work for him. The Egyptians built colossal structures like the pyramids with them. The Greeks used them to refine their architecture to a level that is amazing even today.

Archimedes theorized about machines that used steam for power as early as the third century B.C. Hero of Alexandria, in the first century B.C., wrote about a great range of devices upon which modern machines are based, including the screw, the crank, the camshaft, the cogwheel, the counterweight, the vacuum vessel, the pump, the piston, and the windmill. But there is no evidence that either man saw his ideas turned into working machines. The basic units of work, as in the Egyptian frieze on this page, remained slaves and animals. It would be hundreds of years before the simplest machines came into use and were adapted to devices we now recognize as immediate ancestors of the robot.

Below: The statue's size is colossal. The engineer's problem is how to harness enough manpower to move it, and how to make the slaves work efficiently as a unit. Lewis Mumford refers to this type of human work force as the megamachine.

Right: Heat transfer is what made this Egyptian automaton work. The fire heats the water and turns it into steam. The steam causes the arms of the figures to move and then condenses back into water, which the figures pour on the fire. The drawing is nineteenth century; whether the device actually existed is doubtful.

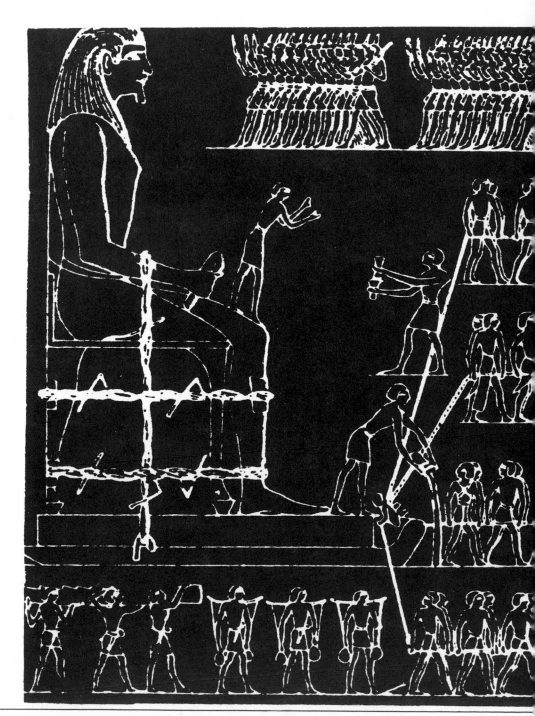

Right: This mechanism used for opening temple doors is a primitive example of a power train. The fire makes the air in the chamber below expand, forcing water into the bucket. As the bucket descends, it pulls the ropes, turning the rollers that open the doors. When the fire is put out, the air contracts, sucking the water back into the chamber. The counterweight closes the doors again, not unlike the mechanism that drives the automatic doors in today's supermarkets. The inventor was Hero of Alexandria.

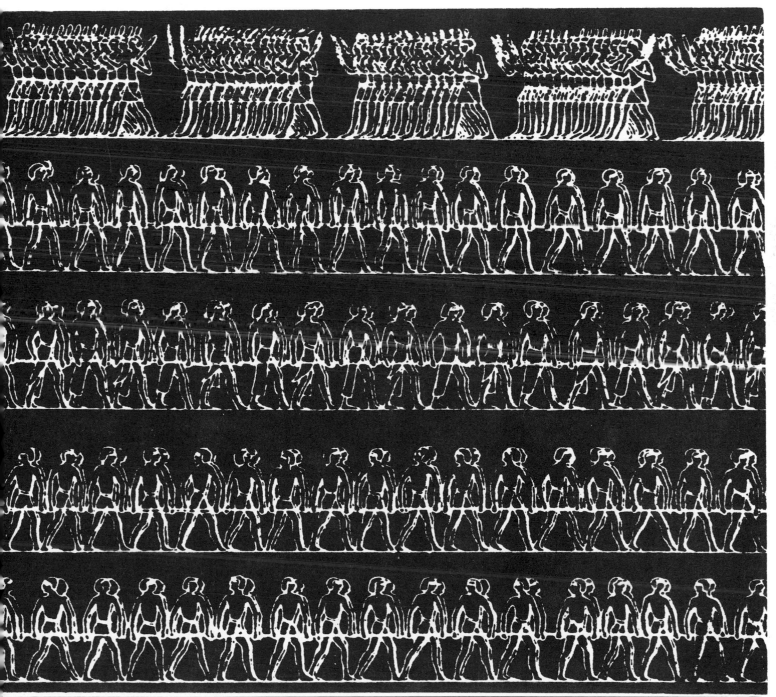

In the Middle Ages, a whole new class of creatures began to appear. At first they were connected with the clocks on churches, town halls, and courtly buildings. Birds, animals, people, they all derived their power from the mechanisms of the clocks, and they all could perform an entire sequence of motions. These new creatures came to be called automatons.

Other automatons derived their power from water or wind. Their mechanisms were the creation of highly skilled craftsmen who combined the talents of the smith, the armorer, the sculptor, and the engineer. The gears, springs, trip levers, and rods that made them move could extend a great distance from their power source, creating the illusion that they moved by themselves.

Some automatons could ring bells, pour water, and do other real work. This functionality led to distinction that exists even to this day, between the humanoid robot that reminds us of the way human beings look and the robot that is a substitute for something a human being does. The difference, for example, between C-3PO and R2-D2 in *Star Wars*.

Clock tower figure. Musée des Beaux-Arts, Strasbourg, France.

Above: The clock atop the cathedral in Strasbourg has been made over twice, each time more elaborately. But it all began with this cock, which first crowed around 1350. Every day at noon it would flap its wings, open its beak, thrust out its tongue, and crow in triumph. Opposite: The Arabs were fascinated with fanciful mechanical devices, from flying horses to automatons like this one, built in 1315, which automatically filled and emptied a wash basin. It was described in a book on automatons by al-Jazari, who may have elaborated it from a drawing by Hero of Alexandria. After the user washed his hands, he pulled a lever. In the sequence of motions that followed, the dirty water was drained and the lady poured fresh water into the basin. The device worked on the same principle as the modern flush toilet.

Below: Atop the great clock tower in Piazza San Marco, in Venice, these two giants have been beating time, hour by hour, since 1497.

Right: The clock in Nuremberg's Franenkirche powers this most famous of glockenspiels. A whole troop of figures sound the hours in procession, walking, ringing bells, and playing instruments. The programming devices for this giant music box are basically the same as for all other clockwork automatons, only this one is done on a grand scale.

By the eighteenth century, the industrial revolution was fully under way, with its proliferation of new power sources, new tools, new industry, and new mechanisms. It became possible to create, within a very small space, machinery capable of controlling a whole sequence of actions. With the machinery and power source so compact, the new automatons, if life size, could be made much more complex; simpler ones could be reduced to miniatures. Aided by craftsmen who made clocks, watches, and dolls, the automaton maker brought his own ingenious solutions and meticulous craftsmanship to the simulation of life.

Royalty demanded to be amused, and so it was: craft eclipsed art, novelty overcame insight. It was an age of decor. In France, Vaucanson and the Jacquet-Droz family made exquisite and complicated automatons, while in Germany, E. T. A. Hoffmann wrote a tale about a dancing doll named Olympia whom nobody could turn off.

By the beginning of the nineteenth century, the vogue of the automaton gradually filtered down to the general population. Although certain craftsmen, including the Maillardet family and Carl Farberge, continued to build exquisite and ingenious devices, the more common automatons became, the less fabulous they were.

The excitement lay elsewhere. In 1791, Luigi Galvani had discovered animal electricity, and this new, mysterious, invisible force promised to unlock the secrets of life. In 1816, Mary Shelley visited Neuchâtel, where the automatons made by Jacquet-Droz were on display. In 1817, she wrote *Frankenstein,* and gave the world an image of artificial life gone wrong that still fascinates today.

Left: In 1738, Jacques de Vaucanson fashioned a duck that was said to walk, swim, and flap its wings. When given food, it would appear to chew and swallow it. Later, it would complete the digestive process (note the arrow near the tail). Although in this illustration the duck appears to be self-contained, most other drawings show a large base below, which housed a weight-driven mechanism.

Below: This elegant Swiss lady musician, by Pierre and Henri-Louis Jacquet-Droz, sways and bends with the music, which she plays with all ten fingers. Unlike human musicians, she never makes a mistake.

Opposite: There was a tacit understanding between the creators of automatons and the people who delighted in watching them. In exchange for the incredible wealth of detail in the figures, the audience agreed to forget, for the moment, that they were not real. This agreement at times led to complications. When the Jacquet-Droz showed this figure, which could write any message (as long as it was less than forty characters long), they were arrested and accused of sorcery. The figure is one of the most complicated automatons ever made. The inset picture shows the sophisticated mechanism built into the body of the figure.

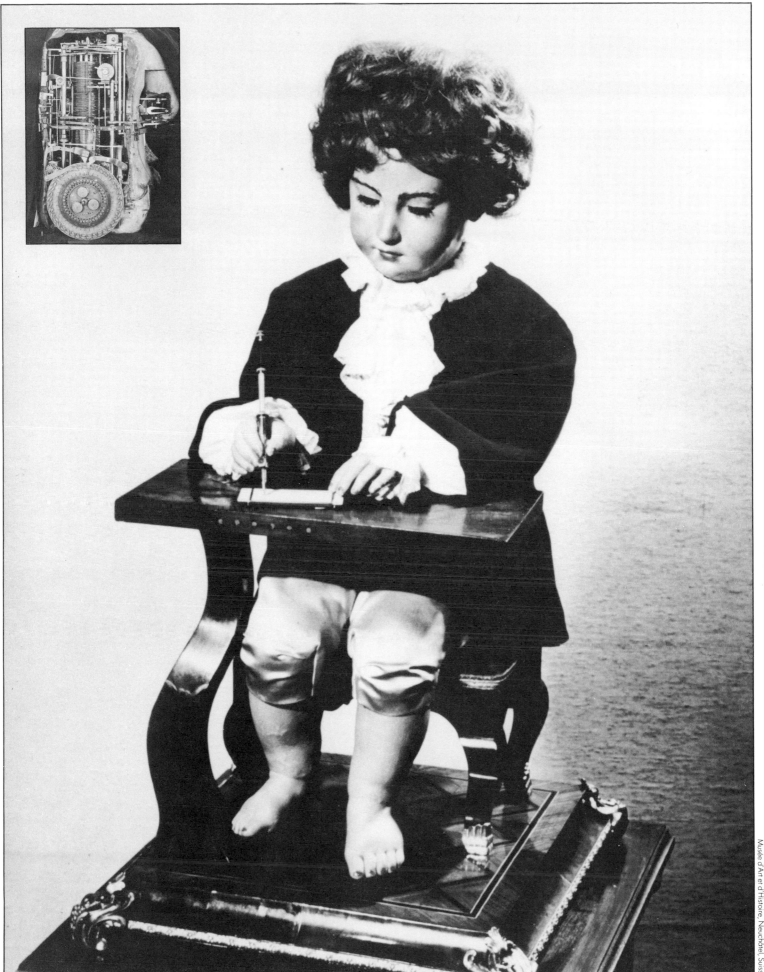

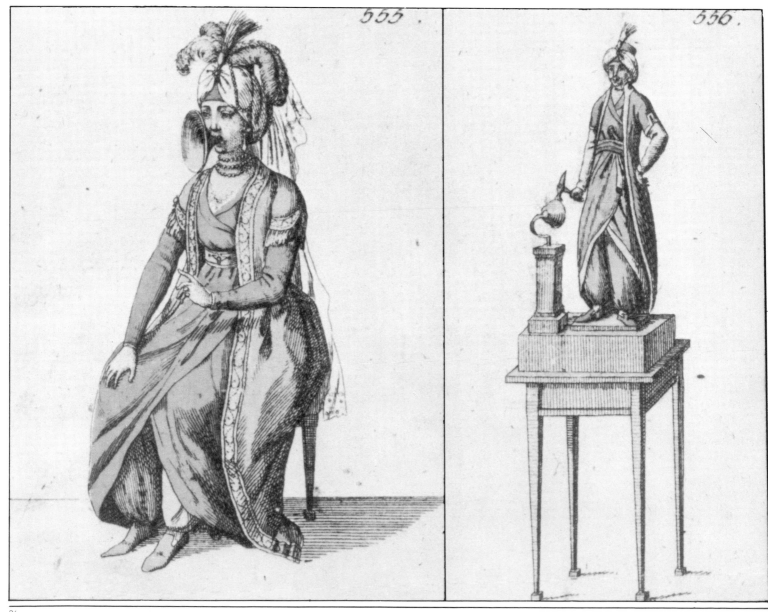

Opposite, top: The automaton has become a toy in this late eighteenth century knife grinder's cart, made in Jouet. Its mechanical linkages are like those commonly used in friction-drive toys today.

Opposite, bottom: Speech was the major obstacle to realistic automatons. During the nineteenth century, inventors tried everything to get their creatures to talk or sing. They tried bellows, vibrating reeds, and diaphragms in small voice boxes. This nineteenth-century Turkish lady made voicelike noises. The gentleman in the picture beside her is a bell ringer, possibly the very first useless domestic appliance for the man who has everything.

Top: "When birds do sing, hey ding-a-ding-a-ding..." Hundreds of these chirping, wing-flapping automatons were made between 1750 and 1930. This one is the work of Von F. Brutmann of Vienna.

Bottom: The notorious 1769 Turk chess player, by Baron Wolfgang von Kempelen. In fact, it is not an automaton at all, but a clever hoax. A dwarf was concealed in the device and did the actual playing—the machinery beneath was an illusion, a magnificent one at that. The spectators of the day wanted so much to believe in it that it was years before the hoax was exposed. Edgar Allen Poe was one of the numerous people who fell for it. When he figured it out later, he did the small inset sketch..

The end of the nineteenth century was the true beginning of the machine age. Machines were everywhere, and people were happy with them. Exposition after exposition was mounted to show off the latest achievements in technology.

Steam powered the large machines. Clockwork powered the small, and it had become extremely reliable and smooth. Pocket watches were common. Soon electricity was to bring a cheap, clean, and versatile source of additional power.

The days of the old-fashioned automaton were clearly numbered. Some were shown at the exhibitions, where they drew crowds of admiring spectators. But the combination of crafts that it took to make them, as well as anyone willing to put out the money to pay for one, was harder and harder to find.

What replaced the automatons were mass-produced dolls and toys. Edison was able to adapt his phonograph to fit inside a rather small doll, and the production of his factory could barely keep up with the demand. Other toys and novelties driven by clockwork proliferated.

Everything seemed to move by itself. Factory owners were busy trying to figure out new applications for the obedient and powerful generation of machines that electricity brought. And, since there seemed to be a machine that could do anything, why not one that could do everything—a robot?

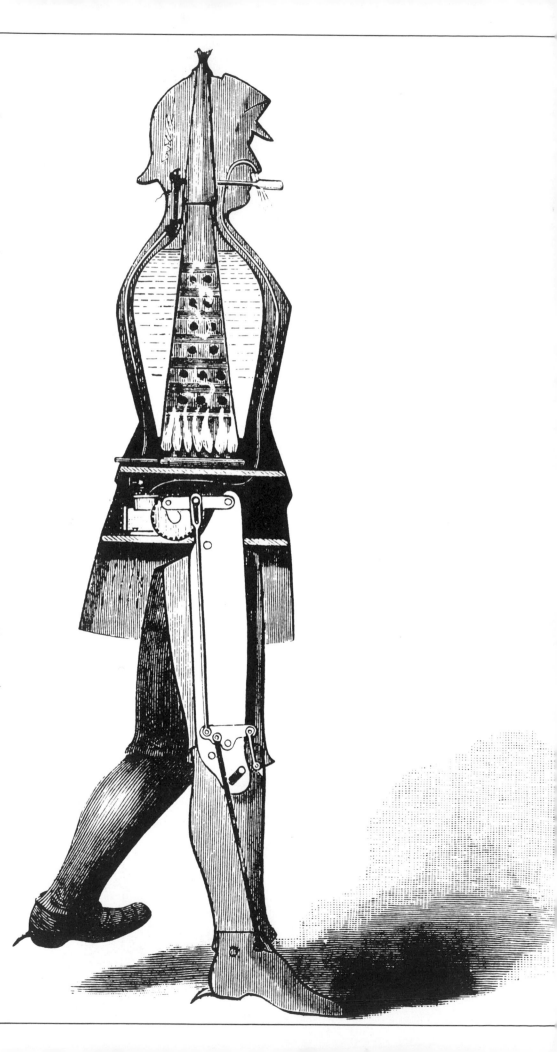

Opposite: This tin man was invented late in the nineteenth century. When he developed a head of steam, he could walk, but only in circles, since he was attached to a horizontal radius arm. Besides being noisy and underpowered—he could develop only half a horsepower—he had a tendency to blow his stack.

Right: When he was not busy inventing the phonograph and the light bulb, Thomas Edison turned his mind to more playful objects. One of them was this phonographic doll, which he perfected in 1894. For the first time, automatons were not a plaything of the rich. The sophistication of the machinery lay in its simplicity and its reliability. It permitted Edison to turn out 500 of them a day at his New Jersey factory.

Below: As novelties at the 1876 World's Fair, these automatons by Maskelyne and Cooke played to a large and enthusiastic public. They were among the last examples of performing automatons in the tradition of the Jacquet-Droz.

While the humanoid automatons were being perfected, useful ones had not been forgotten. What had been theory for Hero became engineering for the Persians, who experimented extensively with harnessing wind and water power, and actually built numerous types of machines at a time when Europe was mired in the Dark Ages. During the Renaissance, Leonardo da Vinci filled notebook after notebook with the solutions to mechanical problems that would later become the backbone of future industrialization.

The globe was proved round, and once again the shape of the world changed. Columbus discovered a new world on the other side of the Atlantic; Vasco da Gama discovered a new ocean on the other side of Africa. Magellan finally circumnavigated practically the whole thing, but did not live to describe its vastness. Suddenly there was an inexhaustible supply of room and of raw materials.

The world was colonized, then industrialized. First the loom, then the whole factory was mechanized. Machines drew power from anywhere it could be found—wind and water first, then steam. The pace of industrialization and technological innovation began its mad acceleration to the pace of today.

Battery and dynamo lighted the streets of cities and ran the motors in factories. The skyscraper went up next to the penny arcade. People ate at the Automat. The machines were there to be loved; it was hard to see how people had ever gotten along without them. From the trolley to the motor car, they changed the face of the world.

Above: The Greeks reasoned that the wind was a powerful force, but it was the Persians who harnessed it. This horizontal windmill, described about 1300 by Al-Dimashqi, predates the first known practical European one by a good 250 years. The sails below rotated a vertical shaft, which turned the stone above. The grain was fed to the stone from a hopper.

Opposite: The shape a machine takes depends on what makes it go and what it is supposed to do. This Persian machine for drawing water uses donkey power and demonstrates graphically how a single machine can do the work of many humans.

Left: Before Edmund Lee invented this system in 1745 for keeping the vanes of a windmill facing into the wind, windmills could be used only when the wind was blowing in the right direction. The principle of automatic self-correction is called feedback, and is an essential aspect of modern technology and of robotic devices.

Below: Jacquard's 1804 industrial loom could automatically weave a pattern into cloth. His system used punch cards to control each pass of the shuttle. Jacquard's invention employed principles that were not far removed from those basic to the digital computer.

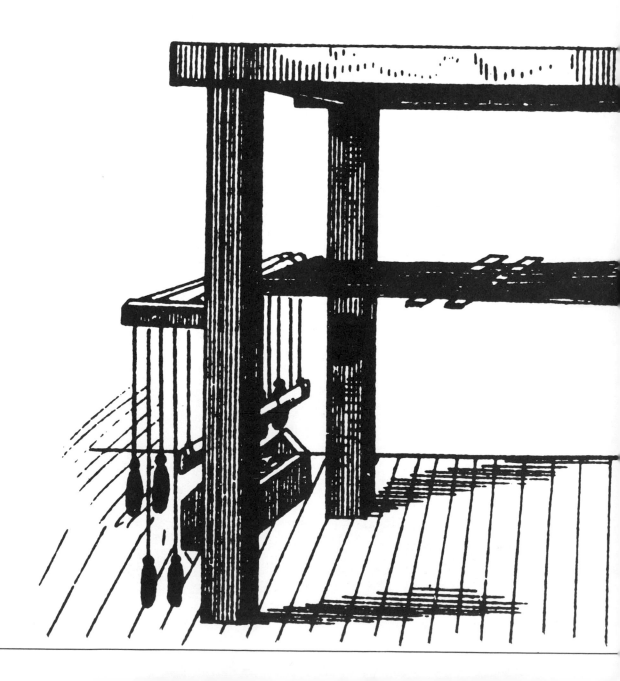

Right: In this early battery-operated vending machine, the candy is on top, the batteries below. In the futuristic film *Alphaville,* Jean Paul Belmondo stops at a vending machine; when he deposits ten francs, the machine issues him a card that says "Thank you."

Below: The unmarked fencer in this 1897 cartoon is a robot. His human opponents are in various states of disrepair. It is not clear whether Hans Hubernauch was proposing an automated way to get your duelling scar, or whether his satire was aimed at the German ruling classes as represented by the fencers.

Opposite: The U.S. Patent Beam Engine was the King Kong of machines at the Philadelphia Centennial Exposition of 1876. Size has always been a symbol of sheer power. The object between the two huge cylinders is called a ball governor. Governors, as well as thermostats, circuit breakers, voltage regulators, power steering, automatic pilots, and photoelectric cells, are among the many feedback devices in common use today.

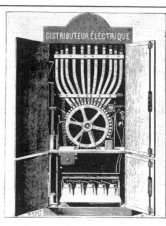

R.U.R. had its premier performance in Prague, Czechoslovakia, in 1921. It was a time when human nature had begun to develop a bad reputation.

World War I had left Europe in an unparalleled state of devastation. It had been a four-year proof of the obstinacy and stupidity of powerful men. It had also represented a significant demonstration of the superior durability of machines over men. Although both sides had consumed material at an incredible rate, there always seemed to be another tank, another shell, another bullet to send against the enemy.

Humans were expendable in that war. Casualties and fatalities had so far outstripped the most terrible estimates that it seemed as though humanity itself might be dispensable.

Capek's robots were manufactured for profit, as a replacement for workers. At first they lacked all human emotion. They represented a conservative's dream solution to the active labor movements and the socialism burgeoning throughout Europe. But Capek was sure that the act of working itself had something humane to fit. As an "improvement," the robots were fitted out with certain human emotions to make them work better. And they do. But then they revolt, turn against their creators, and eradicate them. As the play ends a robot couple emerges as the machine age Adam and Eve.

Capek's play was widely produced outside Czechoslovakia. Five years later, robots were brought to the screen by Fritz Lang. Maria, the evangelistic robot in *Metropolis*, goes off the track. She has the opposite effect from the one her creator intended, inciting the workers to revolt and almost causing a catastrophe.

The robots in *R.U.R.* and *Metropolis* served to crystallize the fear and mistrust some people had—and many people still have—in the changing values of the machine age. The message was clearly that the future was too important to entrust to machines.

Above: Radius is the robot's name. The woman is Helena, and this confrontation is from *R.U.R.* In this first New York production, in 1922, Sylvia Field was Helena and Albert Van Dekker was Radius. The play ran at the Garrick Theater for 184 performances, to mixed reviews. However much the play may have lacked as drama, it made an immediate, indelible impression through the sheer power and originality of its ideas.

Right: Karel Capek, the author of *R.U.R.*

Opposite: The play was as much a comment on the life of workers as it was about robots. Alquist, the clerk in the robot factory, is allowed the dubious honor of being the last human to die, because the robots regard him as the worker who most resembles themselves.

Above: Maria, the wrathful robot from Fritz Lang's monumental film *Metropolis* (1926), was not content to destroy humanity. She wanted to punish it first.

Right: The symbol of artificial life was electricity. Here Maria is being duplicated by the mad scientist, using electricity at high tension. Lang's images, inspired by his first visit to New York City, became prototypes for science fiction and horror films for fifty years after.

SCIENCE

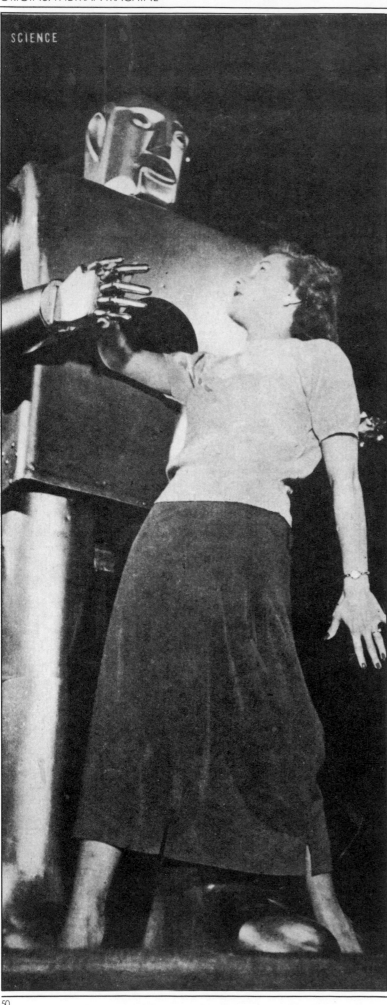

Left: Your average robot seems more primitive than he actually has to be. This one, vintage 1950, was named Electro. His face seems to have been derived from the massive sculpted heads on Easter Island. He could count to ten, smoke, and deliver a speech. The reaction of the sweater girl is straight out of "Beauty and the Beast."

Above: Alpha, a female robot of great pulchritude, amazed the British public in the 1930s with such feats as rising from her chair and answering questions put to her by spectators. There was some speculation that Alpha was bugged, and that the questions were actually answered offstage via a remote microphone. Alpha weighed two tons and was said to smoke a pack of cigarettes a day, perhaps to keep her weight down.

Opposite: The first metal men were tin soldiers. This overgrown example sported rivets for ornamental buttons and stood tall enough to impress his young admirers in Atlantic City.

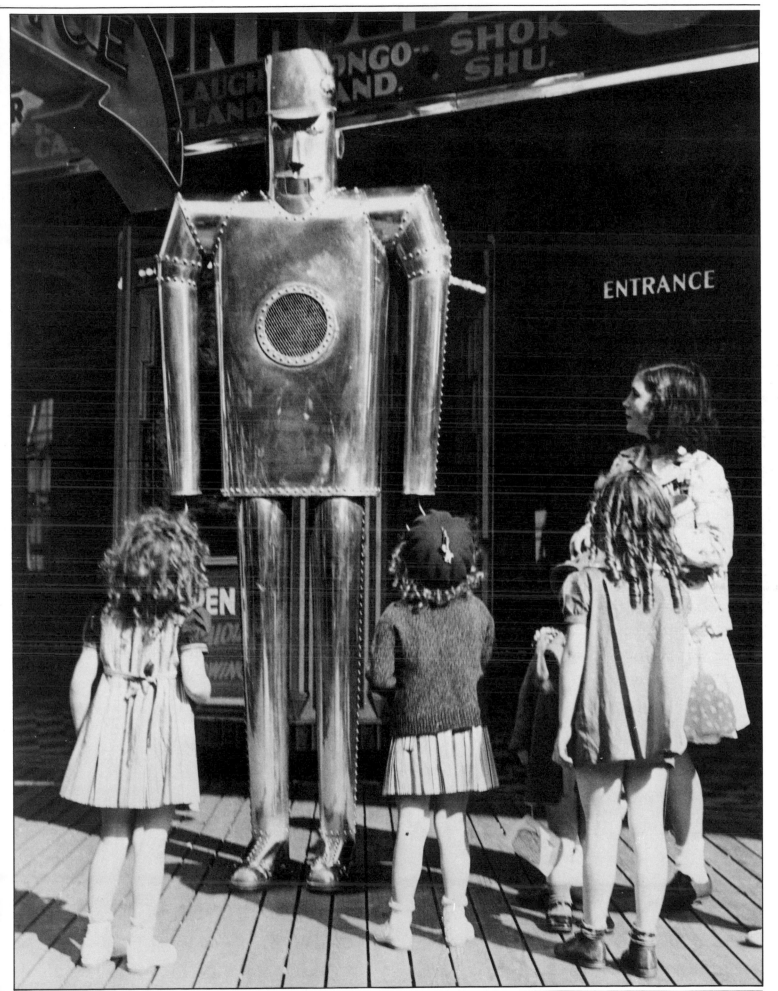

3. ROBOT AS HERO-VILLAIN

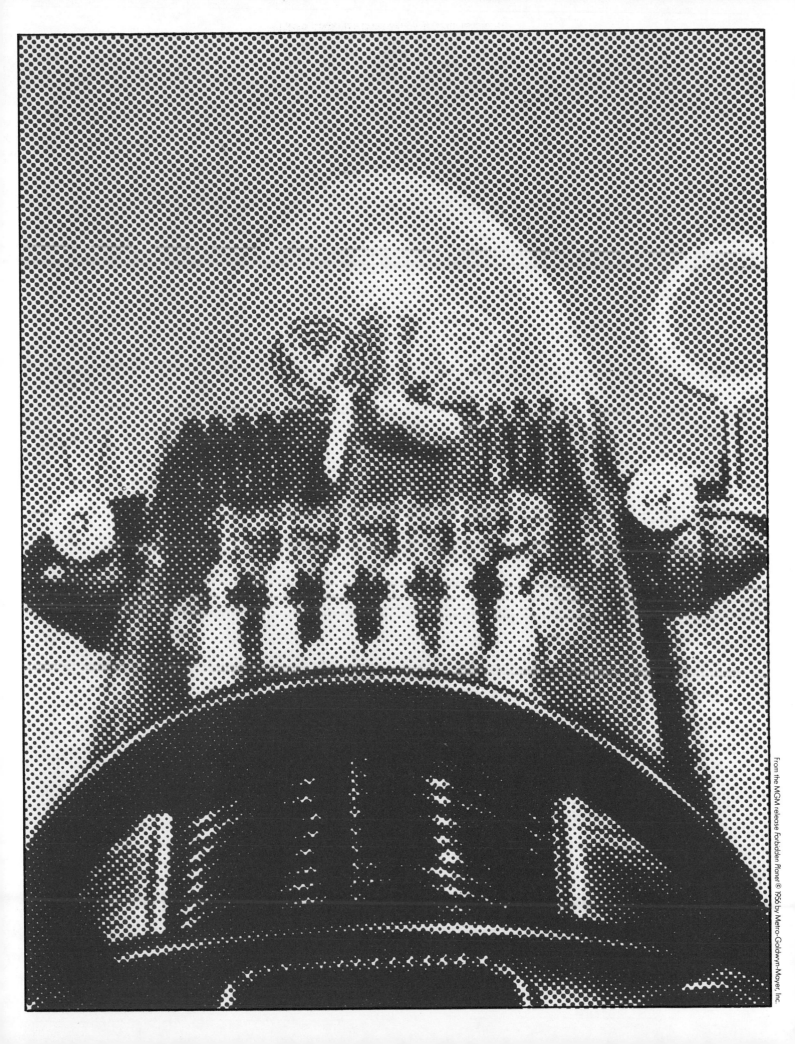

As always, literature took the baton from science and forged ahead. The visionary fiction of Jules Verne described every possibility just beyond the capability of technology, from submarines to rockets, from the center of the earth to the moon. Although there was an inevitable "good-to-be-home" feeling about Verne's endings, there was no disguising the pleasure he felt in the adventure of the journey.

Verne's faith in technology was embraced, at the end of the last century, by H. G. Wells, an English writer. Wells brought the galaxy and the future into the realm of subjects to be explored. Even though they could not be reached by airplane or rocket yet, they could be and were on paper.

The establishment of pulp magazines gave robots a continuous forum. Hugo Gernsback, who coined the name *science fiction* and the word *scientification* to describe what he was doing, wrote *Ralph 124C41+*. His magazine, *Amazing Stories,* was the showcase for an increasing number of contributors. Among them was Abraham Merritt, whose story "The Moon Pool" featured an alien automaton two years before Capek coined the word *robot.*

If Gernsback can be said to have founded science fiction, the man responsible for its coming of age was the late John W. Campbell. In the pages of *Astounding Stories,* which later became the magazine *Analog,* he published the writers who later came to be the greats of science fiction.

Perhaps the most prolific of his contributors, and one of the best, was Isaac Asimov. A scientist, he wrote about what he considered to be the problems of the future, and one of the most serious of them was what to do about robots. He devised a code, called robotics, that governed the robots about which he wrote. His robots were the ancestors of Robby, from *The Invisible Boy,* the drones of *Silent Running* and, of course, the charming and courageous C-3PO and R2-D2 of *Star Wars.*

Above: Isaac Asimov.
Opposite: The pulp magazines, with their tradition of overstatement, did a lot to set the style for robots. In this illustration for a story by Robert Sheckley, the giant robot is glowing with radiation. The power of the technology he represents seems to dwarf our institutions, even Congress.

FUTURE
SCIENCE FICTION

ANC.

25¢

CHARTERED

ALEX

ULTIMATUM!
by ROBERT SHECKLEY

ALL STORIES NEW

A
DOUBLE-ACTION
MAGAZINE

World War I was more than just a killer of humanity. It also killed a way of looking at the world that had been dominant since the Renaissance. The world of formal gardens, grand palaces, ornate public buildings, operas, and bands in the town square vanished overnight. So did fixed lives and a rigid class structure.

Replacing this world was a circus of technological advances. Fast cars, crack trains, air travel, typewriters, phonographs, skyscrapers, and submachine guns. People were polarized into those who reveled in it and those who censured it. Prohibition was enacted. Crime became organized. It seemed to the pessimistic as though the order of the world had come apart. Many were ready to blame it on technology.

The pages of the pulps were filled with metal monsters, all of them getting bigger, less manageable, ready to devour humanity. Most of the time they could be fended off with ingenuity, but the risk was always present that the robot would succeed in wiping out man.

Perhaps the best pulp story, written by John Campbell, was called "The Voice of the Void." It was about a world of ultraphysics and combined Campbell's fascination with technology with the anxiety it aroused in him. It was not the progress of society, but the recklessness that bothered him. The X-Ray could lead to the death ray.

Above: The robots of the pulp magazines reflected the imagination of their day. This cover illustration of Abraham Merritt's "The Metal Monster" looks like a stylized statue, almost Egyptian. The head is reminiscent of the Indian on the Pontiac hood emblem of the 1950s.

Right: Even though the giants in Edmond Hamilton's cover story "The Metal Giants" are clearly robots, the biceps and triceps are oddly human. Hamilton was a very prolific writer and became one of Hugo Gernsback's regulars.

Opposite: Artist Frank R. Paul grew famous by capturing the essence of the science fiction stories he illustrated. The robots in John W. Campbell's "Voices of the Void" were clearly all machine, with their cubic heads and triple hydraulic lower appendages.

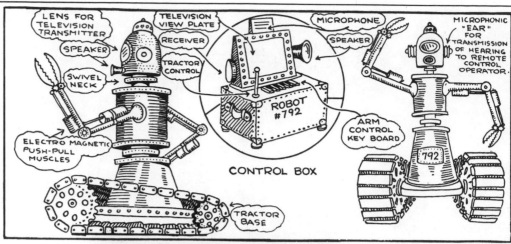

In *Erewhon*, published in 1872, Samuel Butler predicted that machines, through a process of mechanical evolution, would develop cognitive faculties and make slaves of men. By the thirties, it was clear that this idea needed modification—there had been several generations of machines, and they seemed no closer to taking over. But something else was happening that brought the metaphor of the machine to the mind of many writers. The dictators of Europe were glorifying the ability of their subjects to march in locked step and to work like slaves for the glory of the state. The symbol of the machine taking over began to turn up in one futuristic story after another in America and Britain.

In 1928, technology had finally found a positive voice. Philip Nolan wrote a story called "Armageddon 2419 A.D." for Gernsback. It introduced Anthony Rogers. Rogers had been placed in suspended animation by radioactive gas, and woke up 500 years later. As Buck Rogers, he became a star of books, comics, radio, and films throughout the thirties. Always ahead of its time, the Buck Rogers strip predicted atomic energy, jet packs, rocket ships, space travel, and an entire catalog of future technology.

Naturally there were robots in Buck Rogers too. They looked a lot like many of the robots industry now uses in processing radioactive material.

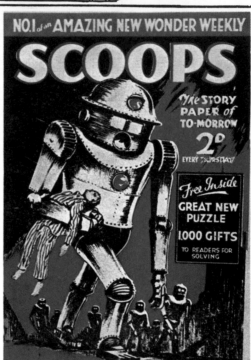

Above: This robot from a *Buck Rogers* strip was drawn by Dick Calkins. It uses the same principles—television, sound pickup, tractor treads, and remote control—as do such real working robots as Mobot I and Mobot II, in service today.

Left: This first number of *Scoops* is from November 1934. The image is very militaristic, and the boiler-plate figures reminiscent of World War I.

Opposite: It is easy to see the Frankenstein association in this illustration by S. R. Drigin from "Menace of the Metal Men," by A. Prestigiacomo, published in *Fantasy Magazine*.

THE RED MAGICIAN: By John Russell Fearn

FANTASY

1/-

THRILLING SCIENCE FICTION

Amazing Scientific Romance
MENACE OF THE METAL-MEN
And Other Great
Imaginative Adventures
By
JOHN BEYNON J.E.GURDON
ERIC F.RUSSELL P.E.CLEATOR
and others.

If World War I meant the death of an old way of life, World War II meant the death of the technology that preceded it. War became too complicated to be fought by two lines of men facing one another on a field. Guns were so powerful that they spread death beyond the horizon. Planes could land on ships, and submarines could prowl for days beneath the surface of the sea. Many of the things that had been speculations on the pages of *Buck Rogers* and *Mechanix Illustrated* became realities—the jet engine, long range rockets, the transistor, plastic, and, of course, the atom bomb.

After the war there was no letup in technological development. At MIT, Norbert Wiener was hard at work on his early concepts of a new science—cybernetics. Claude Shannon developed his information theory. And ENIAC, the first digital computer, the "electronic brain," was born. It was soon followed by increasingly sophisticated computers and, although they were as big as buildings, the dream was already there of a brain that you could put into your pocket, or build into your machine, or even your robot.

Given the probability (more than the possibility) that there would be robots, Isaac Asimov formulated his Three Laws of Robotics: (1) A robot may not injure a human being or through inaction allow a human being to come to harm; (2) A robot must obey the orders given it by human beings, except where such orders would conflict with the First Law; (3) A robot must protect its own existence, as long as such protection does not conflict with the First or Second Laws.

This code of robotic behavior covered the possibilities so well that the actions of virtually all robots who came after—whether or not they had been invented by Asimov—related to them in one way or another. It was one of the first attempts to project laws concerning a morality that was relevant only to the future.

Left: The threat of war, and the fear that the enemy's technology was better than ours, put robots to a new use. In the story "Adam Link Fights a War" Adam Link constructed his robots for peaceful purposes, but when the enemy invaded the United States via Mexico, he mobilized them for war. The illustration is by Fuqua.

Below: One of the constant arguments against technological progress is that humans will get "soft" and, of course, decadent because machines are doing the work for them. The robots here are protecting humans plugged into dream machines. The question is: who is running the machine?

Opposite: Americans and their allies found robots an effective metaphor for the kind of obedience the dictators glorified. Here, the robot is Japanese, the mad creator is Hitler. The seediness and racial slurs testify that this was propaganda in high gear and low taste.

Asimov understood that a brain is a brain, electronic or human, and that brains are in delicate balance, subject to malfunctions and breakdowns. His *I, Robot,* published in 1950, was a testimony to the age of Freud. It featured Susan Calvin, a robopsychologist whose specialty was setting the variables in a robot's "positronic" brain and thereby governing its behavior. The stories worked through the social and psychological complications of human-robot relationships.

Asimov was the thinking robot's man, and, thanks to him, robots enjoyed higher repute for the rest of the decade. Hollywood turned out a seemingly endless series of grade B pictures, trying to fit the formulas of the past onto the subjects of the future. Most of these films were dismal, but a few have made it to posterity and appear now and then on afternoon television. Two of these are *Forbidden Planet* (1956) and *The Invisible Boy* (1957). The robots in these movies were as essential to the action as the humans they served.

If everybody had been as enlightened as Asimov, technology might have followed a more humane, more sensible direction. But in 1952, with the explosion of the first hydrogen bomb, technology began to get a bad name for itself again.

From the MGM release *The Invisible Boy* © 1957 by Loew's Incorporated.

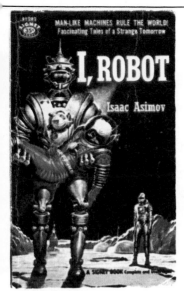

Above: Isaac Asimov was the first to codify the psyche of robots and to recognize that the psychology of a machine might not be quite the same as that of a human being. People who work with real computers have come to recognize a whole range of "psychological" disorders; fatigue is the number one problem. Robots that misunderstood humans became standard science fiction fare.

Opposite: The bionic woman of the fifties was every bit as avant-garde to her age as Jamie Summers is to ours. Note how crude the electronics are compared to the solid-state technology of today.

Opposite, below: Robby the Robot, from MGM's *The Invisible Boy*, was the first of a whole generation of robots whose main occupation was baby-sitting. In this still, the only synthetic objects are the robot and the plastic pitcher—technology at the service of man.

Right: "The Caves of Steel," by Isaac Asimov, appeared in the October 1953 issue of *Galaxy*. It was a robot detective thriller. Against a background of twelve-lane moving sidewalk highways and vast, balconied arcades, the struggle took place between robots, humans, and the bionically in between.

THE CAVES OF STEEL By ISAAC ASIMOV

By the time the fifties were over, the landscape was virtually teeming with robots. The Soviet Union had orbited a Sputnik in 1957. It and the United States were locked into a race to land first on the moon. Suddenly there was a need for robots to replace humans under conditions that humans could not survive.

Robots had already been developed for industrial and scientific use. The combination of video cameras, computers, and precision engineering made them able to perform extremely complicated and delicate tasks reliably. To use them in space, on the moon, or on another planet, was simply a matter of more involved calculations. They became standard equipment.

They were standard equipment in movies and on television as well. Several new series involving space were born, and each one had at least one robot. Some were benign, like the robot baby-sitter of *Lost in Space*; other, more malevolent ones appeared in *Dr. Who* (a British production), *Star Trek,* and the British *Avengers* series.

The robot that fascinated and horrified the sixties was HAL, the computer who schemed for control of the spacecraft in *2001, A Space Odyssey.* HAL was the creation of Arthur C. Clarke, another venerable writer of science fiction, and represented Asimov's robotics gone wrong. Not only did HAL possess a robot's psyche, but he understood human psychology virtually as well as did humans themselves. He belonged to a generation of intelligent machines that were so complex that they had been designed and built by intelligent machines themselves. Humans had lost control.

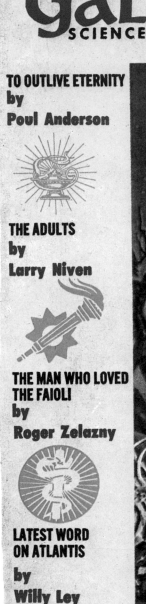

June 1967
60¢

Galaxy
SCIENCE FICTION

TO OUTLIVE ETERNITY
by
Poul Anderson

THE ADULTS
by
Larry Niven

THE MAN WHO LOVED THE FAIOLI
by
Roger Zelazny

LATEST WORD ON ATLANTIS
by
Willy Ley

Above: The threat of nuclear holocaust reached its peak in the sixties. Science fiction writers speculated wildly and daringly about who might survive and what life would be like afterward. Naturally, robots stood the best chance of all.

Opposite: Space colonists would need certain touches of home to be happy. The two puppy lap robots were drawn by Lynx in 1965, several years before Woody Allen's famous Rags was created for *Sleeper.* By the time *Star Wars* was released in 1977, the pet "droids" had lost all similarity to their canine counterparts.

PLUTO

—LYNX—

In our time, robots have come of age. Although there are still a few, like the Fembots in *The Six Million Dollar Man*, who represent the machine at the command of a mad scientist, today's robots are rather benign.

In fact, the man-machine seems rather a tame concept to us. We are no longer afraid of a machine just because it goes trotting across the landscape. We hardly notice machines that speak to us and "understand" what we say to them—we have telephones and computers that can do that.

The robots of our imagination have taken on personality. Most of them lean toward the cool sophistication of the creatures in Woody Allen's *Sleeper*. If they do not achieve quite that degree of panache, they are at least the loyal and courageous creatures of *Star Wars*. Still, they are a little neurotic, as though inbred from too much specialization. They seem to be sadly aware of their own limitations.

It is almost as though the robots had their chance to take over the planet in earlier decades, but failed. In this metaphoric war, humans emerged the victor and went on to domesticate robots, along with all the rest of our machines. From the menace we once imagined robots to be, they have now become our trusted servants. But do we *really* trust them?

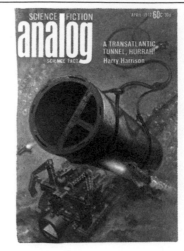

Left: The gap between the real and the possible has narrowed to almost nothing. This robot tunnel builder crawled across the bottom of the Atlantic Ocean in a 1972 story by Harry Harrison. Automatic tunnel diggers, pipeline wrappers, and road builders now in use are similar in concept.

Below: The elegant and rather precious C-3PO and his egg-headed companion R2-D2 turn the tables on those who were afraid that the robots might take over. They need constant cleaning, oiling, and repair. They get confused, distracted, and their feelings are easily hurt. But far beyond their programming, these two robots are overcome by the charm of Luke and Leia, defending and aiding them with what anyone, human or machine, would have to call courage.

Opposite: The robot doing the demolishing is clearly female; the one on the ground is less clearly defined. The rage and destructiveness and the human way they are expressed on this cover from the French magazine *Metal Hurlant* demonstrate that, although we have modified the robots of *R.U.R.* to fit our more sophisticated technology, we have never forgotten their capacity to go wrong.

Star Wars © 1977 Twentieth Century-Fox Film Corporation. All rights reserved.

LES HUMANOIDES ASSOCIES PRESENTENT

METAL HURLANT

Bimestriel
Pour Adultes

NO.8

**SPECIAL ETE
100 PAGES**

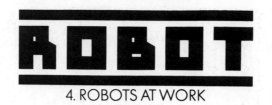

4. ROBOTS AT WORK

A robot that performed real work had to await the development and perfection of several subsystems.

Although articulation and linkages of joints had been possible for a century, a sensitive means of controlling them was lacking. And although electric motors had existed since the last century, it was not until we miniaturized them that we had a size convenient for a working robot.

What really made working robots possible, though, was the development of controls to keep them performing optimally and to make corrections themselves if anything went wrong. Although simple feedback devices had long existed, they could not be used for robots until they could be attached to a computer that could prescribe the correction.

It was not until the fifties that this coming together of all the elements took place. But since then, the development of working robots has been rapid.

Observe a working robot. It does not resemble a human being at all. Its shape is tailored completely to the job it is expected to do. Most of the time, articulation in no way resembles human limbs.

Robots perform tasks for us that we cannot do ourselves. They can be designed to work under conditions that are too hostile or too harsh for humans. They can handle nuclear and other materials too toxic for people to touch. And they can do the kind of heavy, repetitive work that becomes dangerous to humans because it is both tiring and boring.

These working robots represent the flowering of an idea that Norbert Wiener had at the beginning of the fifties: the human use of human beings. Making people perform like machines is thinking backwards. If a job is machinelike, invent a machine to perform it. That machine may cost a person a job, temporarily, but it will never cost that person his or her humanity.

Above: W. Grey Walter's "tortoise" without its shell. Walter called it a Machina Speculatrix and designed its computer to reproduce the behavior of an animal's conditioned reflex. It reacts to and seeks out the source of light.

Left: Not all robots are complicated. Handsome, ever-smiling Silent Sam is a robot flagman. He never tires, never stops for lunch, needs no supervision or health insurance. At six feet and 200 pounds, he replaces a man doing boring, dangerous, and uncomfortable work.

Opposite: In this photograph for display, the Mobot Mark II is holding a Geiger counter. Under real conditions, the counter would be built in, leaving both of its versatile hands free. To permit maximum maneuverability, Mobot's wrist, elbow, and shoulder are double-jointed.

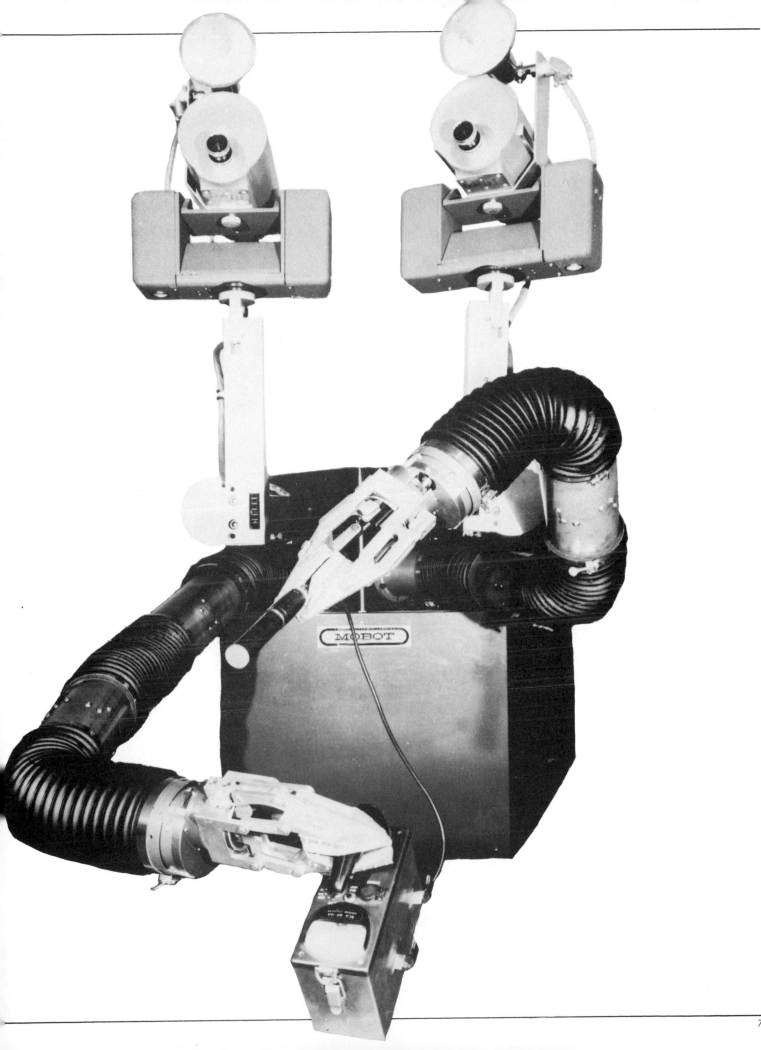

Hunched over an automobile assembly line at General Motors, 20 robots working in tandem put components into position on a car's underbody, then spot weld them. The line is 231 feet long. As the underbody is passed from one robot team to the next, a robot positions the component, while another puts as many as 15 spot welds into precise points. Near the end of the line, a robot checks positioning of the components. Specialized robot assembly lines have also been set up in Italy, Germany, Sweden and Japan.

Opposite: As big as an elephant, this research prototype quadruped built by General Electric engineers is eleven feet tall and weighs 3,000 pounds. The operator uses his legs to initiate movements in the machine's rear legs, and his arms to activate the front legs. Although it can easily kick a 1,500-pound beam across a room, it is perfectly balanced and capable of the most intricate movements.

Right: Exoskeletons are a staple of science fiction. This powered exoskeleton, another product of General Electric, will mimic and amplify any movement of the operator's arms or legs, giving him superstrength.

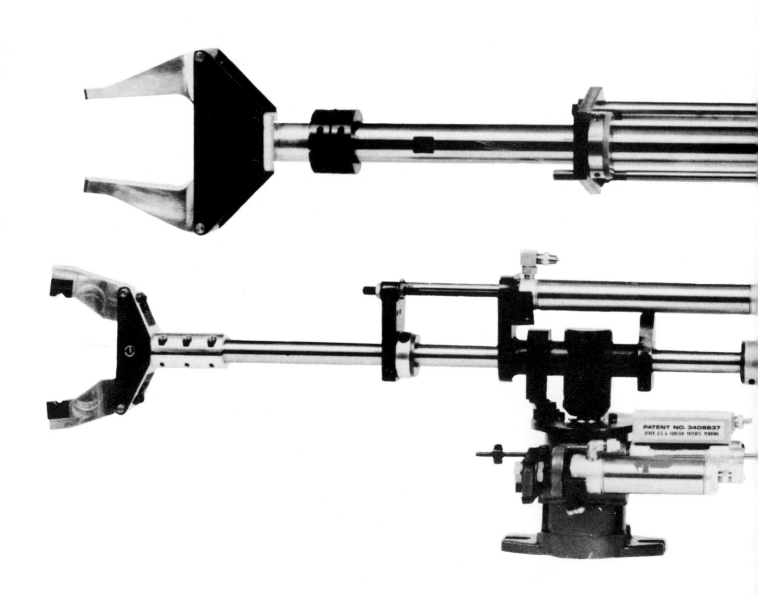

Opposite: The laser beam in this robot by Auto Place is being used to "see" the shape of the metal part being held by its arm. An ingenious system of mirrors guides the laser through and around the holes and slots of the part, then transmits the information to an attached computer, which decides whether the part is acceptable or not. It can measure the accuracy of critical dimension more finely than any human operator could.

Below: The Auto Place robot arm comes in various sizes to fit different jobs. It can move left and right, up and down, extend, contract, and rotate, all the while opening or closing its grip.

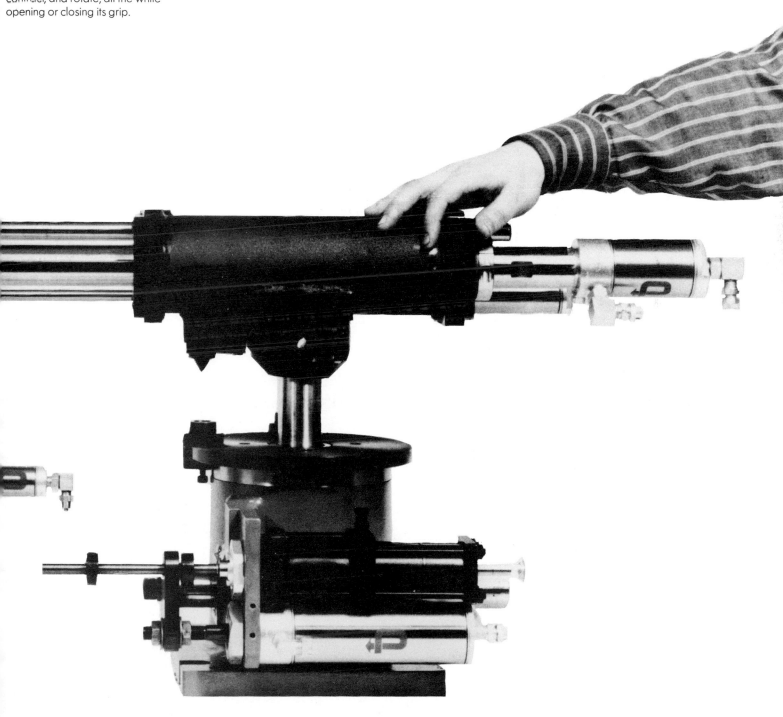

J. F. Engelberger has done more than anyone else to bring robots into industry. Early experimenters who received patents for their research were Tom James and George Devol, but it was Engelberger who got robots built. He began developing industrial models in 1958, and by 1961 was ready to test one in a General Motors plant.

In addition to robots, Engelberger developed a related device that depends on what he calls "telecherics," the amplification by a machine of the movements of a human operator who can bring his own judgment to bear according to the job. Because it senses the action of the operator and imitates it (rather than getting its instructions via buttons or other controls) this device can really be thought of as a robot.

Engelberger calls his robots Unimates. They have already performed more than 7 million man hours of work. Looking ahead, he predicts that robots will have increased manufacturing and service applications and will even find a place in the home. Before this can become a reality, however, designers will have to create robots that are more "human" and able to make sophisticated and delicate decisions based on judgment.

Opposite: J. F. Engelberger with
one of his Unimates. The robot
can be programmed to perform
a complicated work cycle and to
make a limited number of "decisions" on its own.

Above: This ITT Research Institute
robot can be operated by remote control, permitting it to
handle explosives safely.

Right: This General Electric industrial boom is an example of what
Engelberger calls a *telecheric*
device. The operator inserts a
hand and arm into the sensing
apparatus of the machine and
goes through the motions of the
given task. The telecheric machine imitates those motions and
thus performs the task.

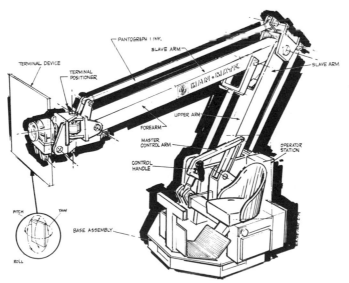

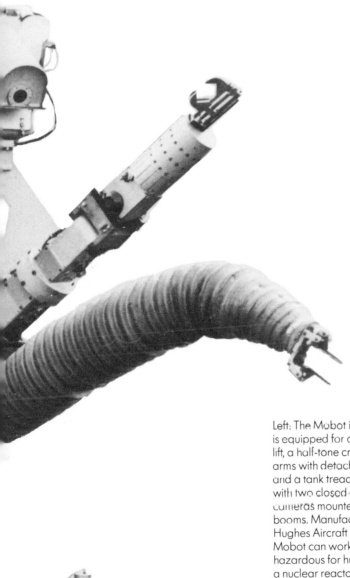

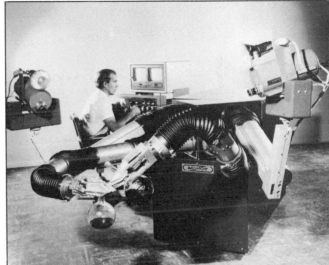

Left: The Mobot industrial robot is equipped for action with a fork lift, a half-tone crane, mobile arms with detachable hands, and a tank tread. It can "see" with two closed-circuit television cameras mounted on flexible booms. Manufactured by Hughes Aircraft Company, Mobot can work where it is too hazardous for humans, such as in a nuclear reactor test area. All of the attachments are accessories. The robot itself is the central mechanism.

Top: Mobot II has padded hands designed to handle tasks as delicate as pouring a corrosive chemical from one flask to another without spilling. The operator remains out of the danger area and guides the robot from a console.

Bottom: This lightweight cousin has a mobile arm and hand that can lift 160 pounds. It was developed by Programmed and Remote Systems Corporation, and represents a very convenient format for medium duty robots.

Opposite: The C130H Link trainer flight simulator, developed by Singer, is an artificially controlled environment, inside which flights conditions are simulated. The machine executes any operation the pilot commands in response to the preprogrammed situation. The impression of being in an actual plane is uncanny. A computer-controlled, widescreen film system reproduces the experience of take-off, flight, or landing. Because this robot furnishes feedback to the humans inside, it can provide a virtually limitless range of flight conditions. It is also the safest and most effective way to train pilots.

Right: Inside the flight simulator, the pilot's orientation is given to him through the instruments. His responses and corrections are executed through the controls. Both pilot and machine respond to feedback. When the corrections are sufficient, the simulated flight appears stable.

One of the simplest robots ever built is the "tortoise," designed in 1950 by W. Grey Walter to simulate conditioned reflexes in animals. The tortoise responds to the stimulus of light in the same way that Pavlov's dog did to the ringing of bells.

Most medical and scientific robot devices are much more complex than Walter's tortoise. The most exciting application is in organ replacement, where devices must be extremely durable and reliable. Then there are bionic limbs, familiar to all in fiction, but now a reality. These prosthetic devices are controlled by the brain of the person equipped with them. Scientists are also working on a scanner that will be able to "see" for blind people. And then there are the life support systems used in hospitals. These are so effective that we have had to rethink the medical and legal definitions of death.

The most complicated robot built so far is the Viking Lander that was sent to Mars in 1976. It is a working laboratory, fully equipped to perform a series of experiments on anything it can reach on the surface of the red planet. As incredibly versatile as it is, it does not begin to approach the complexity of a human being—it is just not in the same league.

Current research in computers, and in robot devices for science and medicine, is so advanced that each generation is obsolete within a few years. And the pace is accelerating. As new areas of investigation, such as genetic engineering, are opened to investigation, science will need ever more able, more intelligent machines.

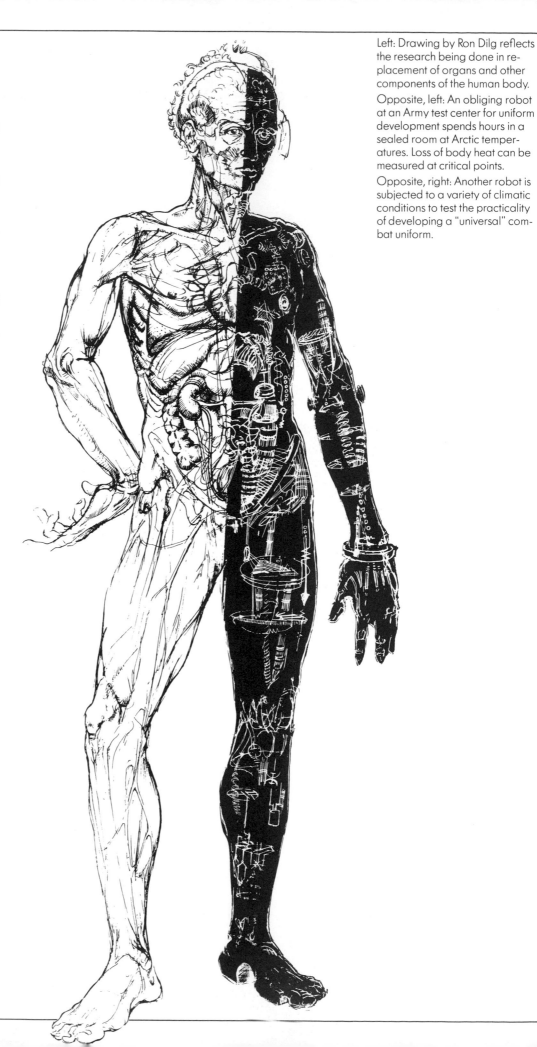

Left: Drawing by Ron Dilg reflects the research being done in replacement of organs and other components of the human body.

Opposite, left: An obliging robot at an Army test center for uniform development spends hours in a sealed room at Arctic temperatures. Loss of body heat can be measured at critical points.

Opposite, right: Another robot is subjected to a variety of climatic conditions to test the practicality of developing a "universal" combat uniform.

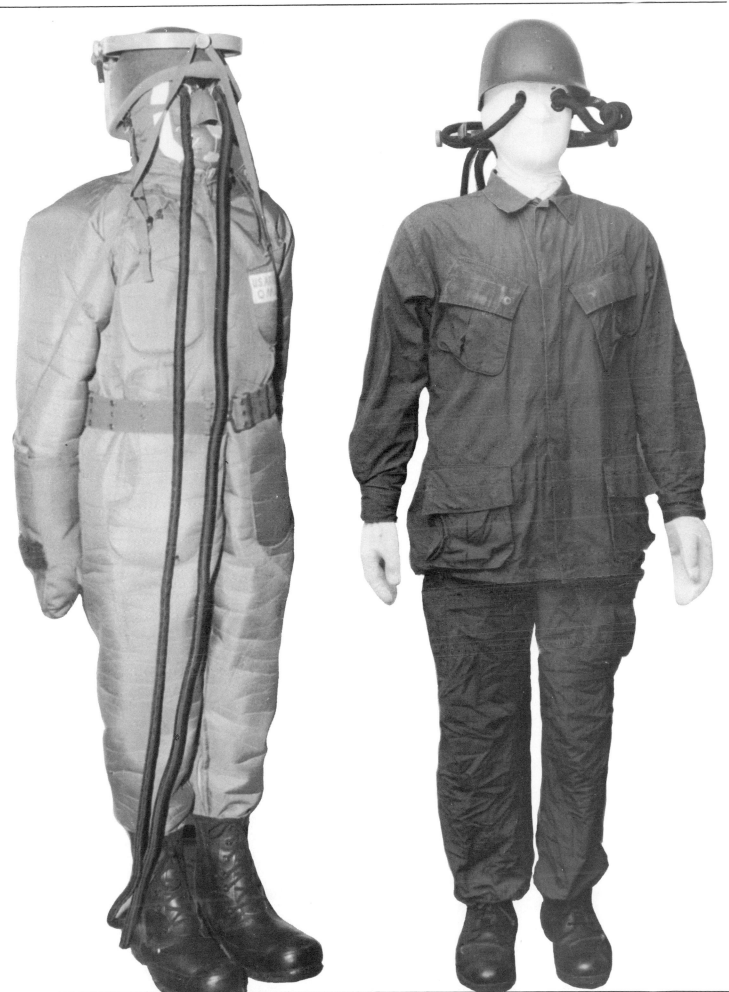

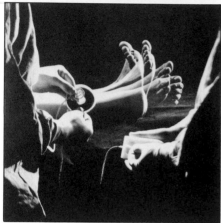

Left, above: Before the pacemaker could be developed, there had to be steel that could be perfectly sterilized, incredibly tiny electrical components, and a long-lasting source of power. Now implanted in the chest of more than 100,000 heart patients, pacemakers provide an electronically controlled pulse to help regulate the patient's heartbeat.

Left, below: Galvani discovered animal electricity in 1791. We are still investigating it. The foot in this picture is reacting to tiny, almost imperceptible electric currents. This research is directed toward treating a nerve condition called "drop foot."

Below: With the Carrel-Lindbergh perfusion pump, organs could be preserved outside the human body for the first time. Developed in 1935, it used pulsating pressure to circulate fluids through the organ without contaminating it. The Lindbergh who codeveloped it is the same Charles Lindbergh who flew the Atlantic solo.

Opposite: Analyzing blood samples by hand is a tricky and time-consuming process. It is enormously simplified and speeded up by this Auto-Analyzer by Technicon, which gives a continuous readout on blood samples it is fed.

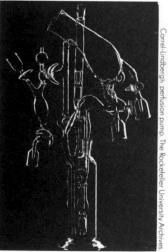

Carrel-Lindbergh perfusion pump. The Rockefeller University Archives.

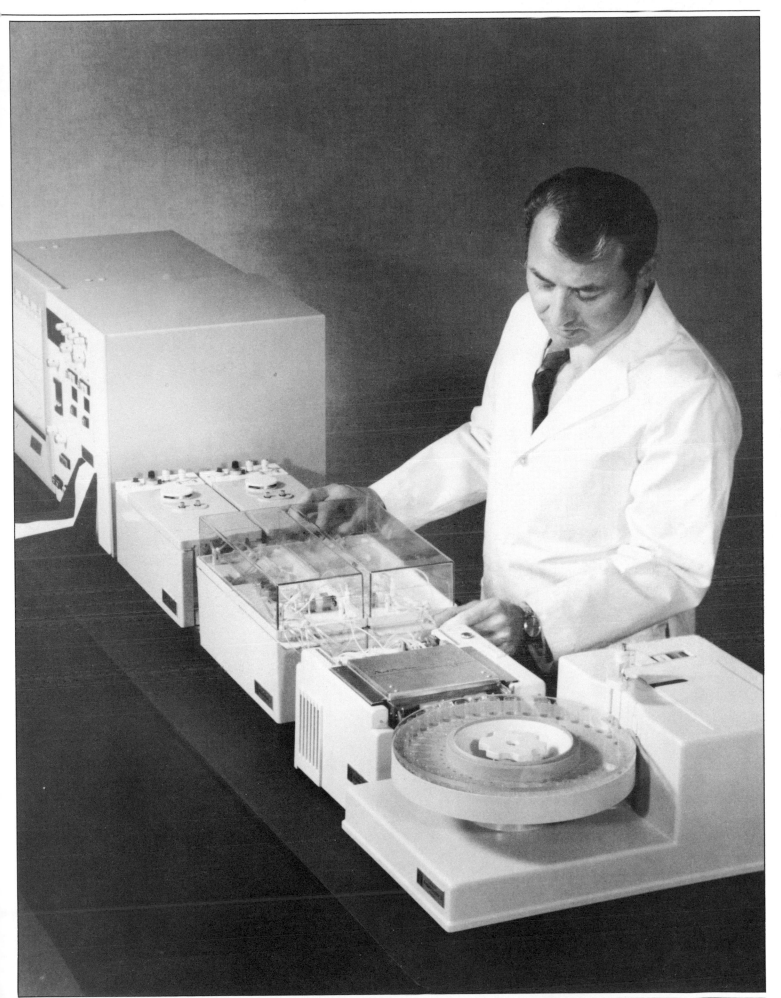

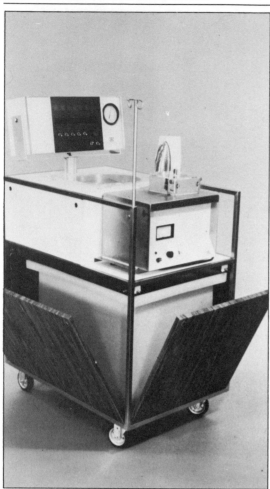

Left: The kidney dialysis machine has literally saved the lives of thousands of people whose kidneys no longer function to cleanse their blood of waste materials generated by the body. In treatments that average three times a week, a patient's blood is circulated through the machine where delicate membranes screen out impurities. This model is manufactured by Baxter Travenol Laboratories, Inc.

Below: Fiction becomes reality in this prosthetic device, developed by the Veteran's Administration. Rather than enhance the power of the wearer's arm, it is designed to function as closely as possible to a normal arm. It is connected to the wearer's neuromuscular system and is commanded by his neurological impulses.

Opposite: This research device is called a head-mounted, eye-marker camera. It records the scene being viewed by a subject and superimposes on it a spot indicating the specific point at which the subject is looking. The device has been used to develop information for improved visual performance.

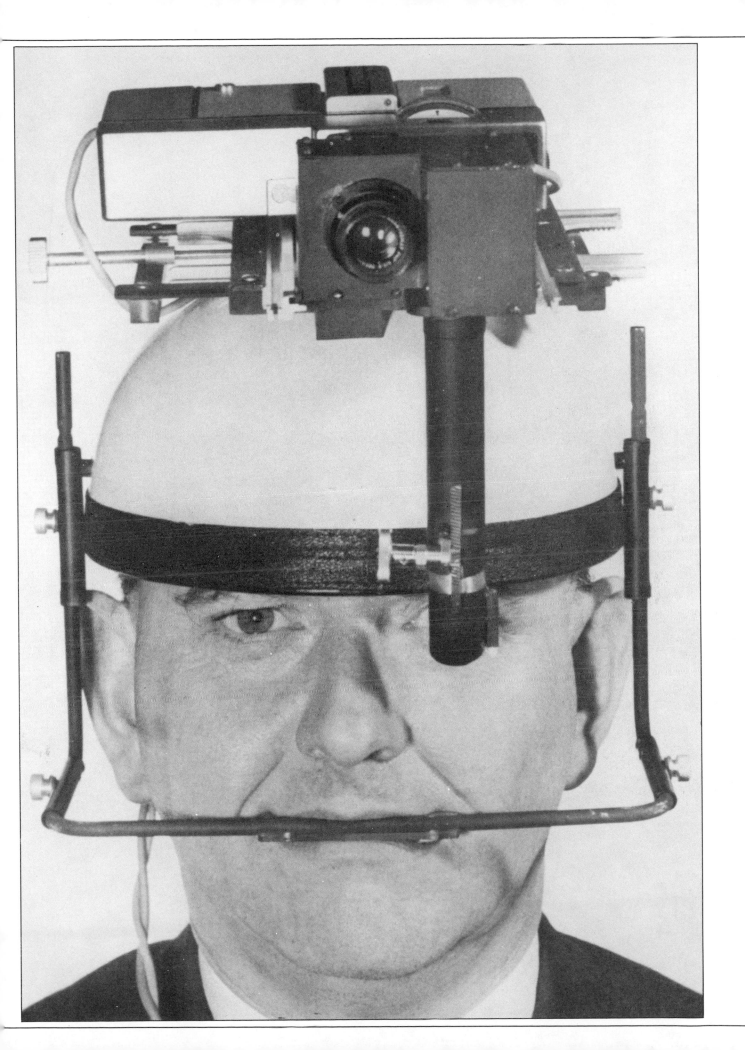

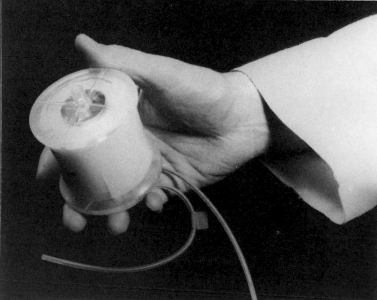

Top left: This heart-assist device was developed by the National Heart Institute and the National Institute of Health. Researchers are testing devices like this in animals preliminary to implanting them in humans. The rotary motion of the pump keeps a continuous flow of liquid pulsing through the valves.

Bottom left: The Kilobow spiral coil membrane functions as an artificial lung. It is one of several mechanisms that doctors are testing for treatment of acute respiratory failure. New plastics and casting techniques bring these assist devices closer to becoming an everyday reality.

Opposite: This X-ray shows an implanted left-ventricular assist mechanism at work. Designed to provide temporary relief to the heart's main pumping chamber, the pump is controlled by timed bursts of compressed air, fed in from outside the body, which flexes the pumping bladder. It was developed by Thermo Electron Corporation and Children's Hospital Medical Center in Boston.

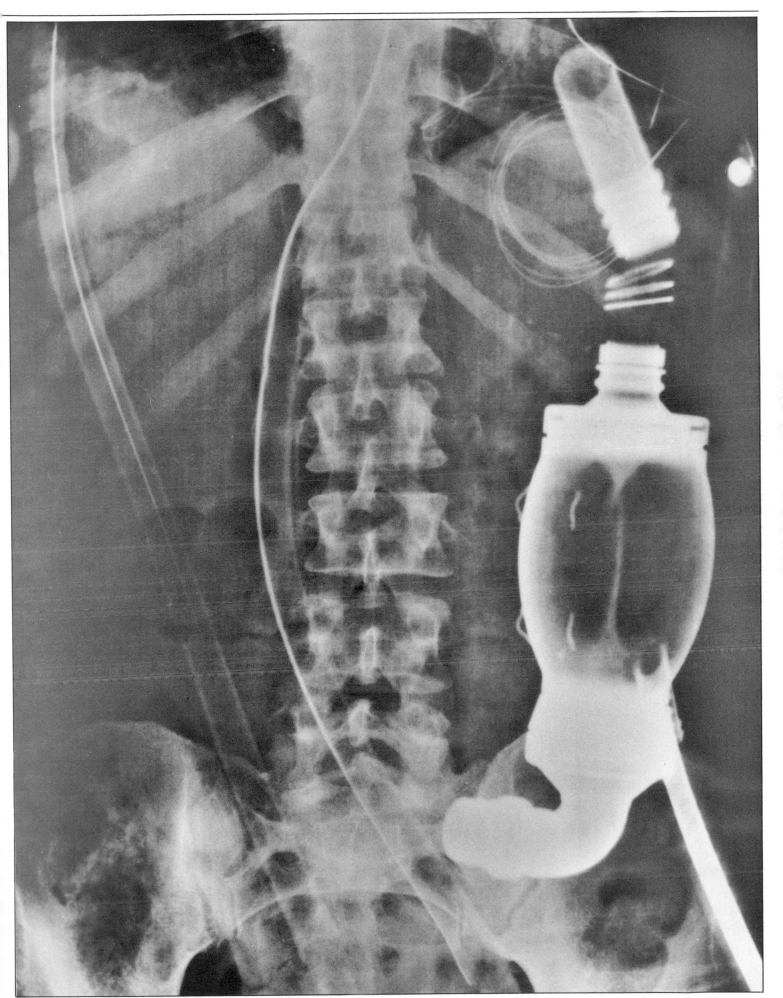

The cliché of the spaceman has been with us for decades in science fiction. When we finally realized manned flight in space, we lionized the astronauts. But now it will probably be decades before we send a human on deep space missions or anywhere but on the most routine orbital flights.

In fact, robots are more efficient and less trouble than humans in space. There is no need to provide them with the elaborate life support systems, "breathing room," and insulation that astronauts need. And for the same weight, as an astronaut, a robot can provide a great deal more reliability and autonomy.

We have put robots on the moon and Mars. Two are on the way to Jupiter and beyond. The resemblance of those robot space travelers to humans is scant, but they do their jobs magnificently, and faithfully report back to us.

Humans will command the newly developed space shuttle. But even on these missions, robots will be used as monitors, backup systems, and maintenance devices. A human will be in the driver's seat, but most of the driving will be done by robot.

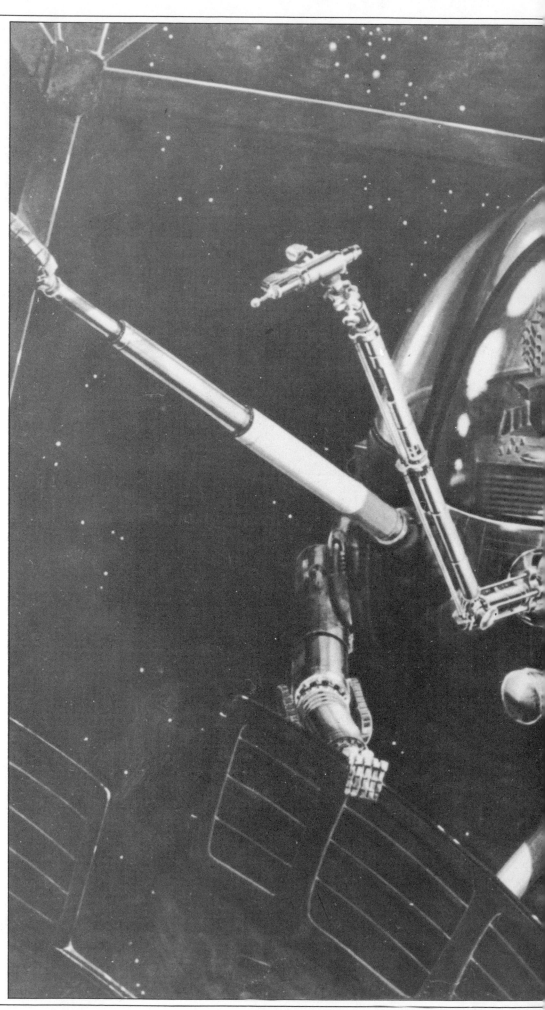

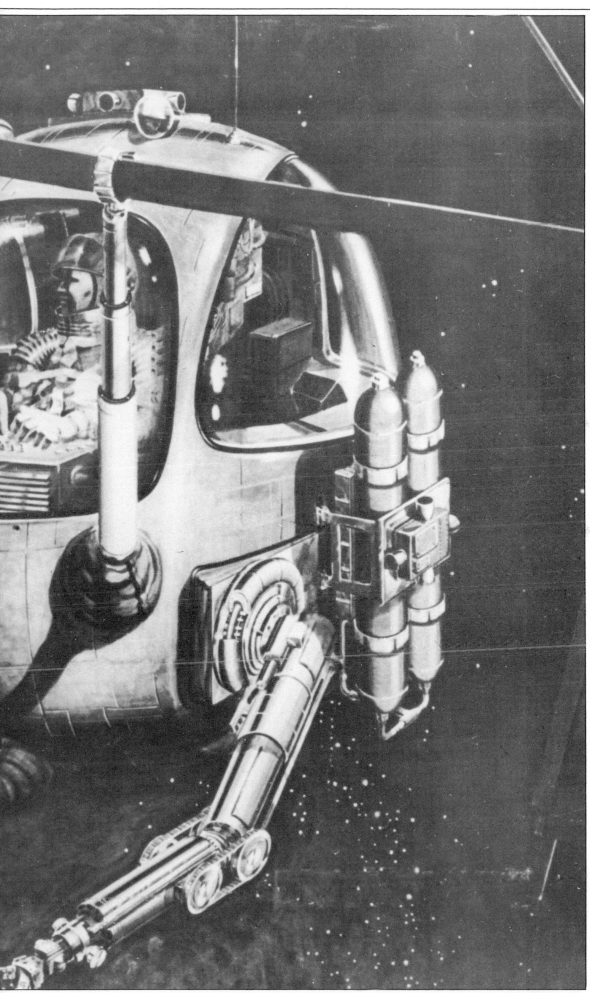

NASA conceived this design for a "space taxi" in 1966. It would be used for construction, repair, and maintenance jobs in space. Although there is room for an operator, the unit could maneuver under its own power by remote control. The number and kind of tools that could be fitted to its arms are virtually limitless. The taxi is reminiscent of the space pod used in Kubrick's film 2001.

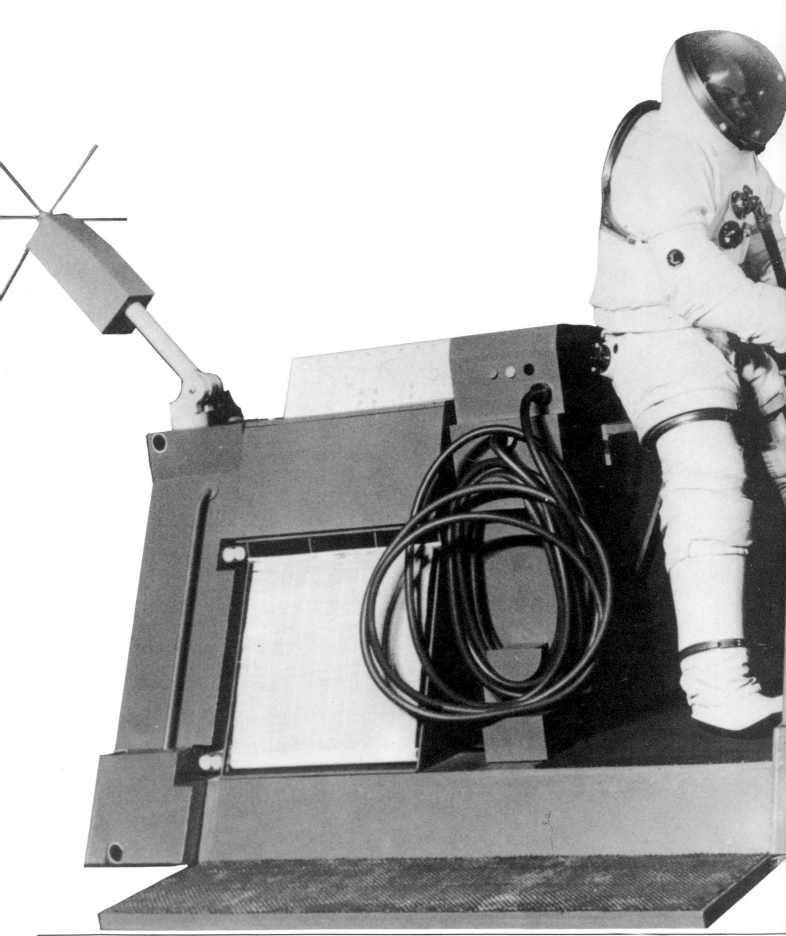

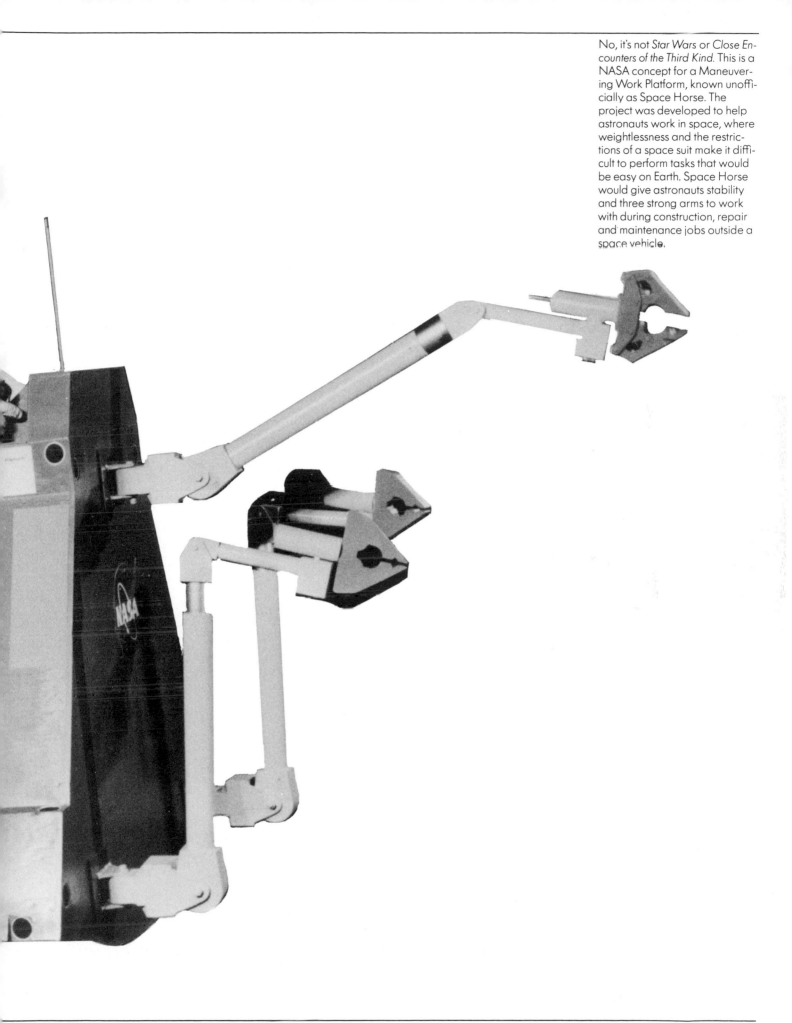

No, it's not *Star Wars* or *Close Encounters of the Third Kind*. This is a NASA concept for a Maneuvering Work Platform, known unofficially as Space Horse. The project was developed to help astronauts work in space, where weightlessness and the restrictions of a space suit make it difficult to perform tasks that would be easy on Earth. Space Horse would give astronauts stability and three strong arms to work with during construction, repair and maintenance jobs outside a space vehicle.

Left: Martin Marietta Corporation designed this Unified Biology Instrument for a future Mars lander, Viking III. A mobile laboratory is intended to survey soil and atmospheric conditions in different locations throughout the Martian year. Viking III would be equipped with eleven test cells to conduct biological and chemical experiments on command.

Below: The Viking I and Viking II landers were the most complex robots ever constructed and proved remarkably dependable. Almost all systems operated according to plan on Mars, and those that did not were repairable in almost every case upon instructions from Earth.

Opposite: Duplicate space vehicles are kept available in case mission control wishes to try out a maneuver on Earth before beaming instructions into space. Here, Viking I demonstrates its long boom arm for collecting soil samples. The samples are deposited in one of three cylinders on the body of the lander for analysis. The lander houses numerous scientific experiments, all conducted by automatic instrumentation.

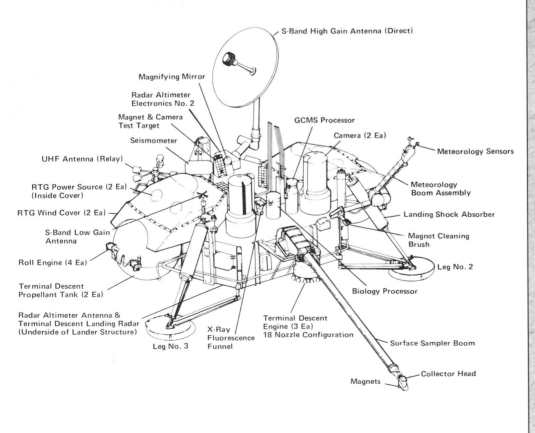

S-Band High Gain Antenna (Direct)

Magnifying Mirror

Radar Altimeter Electronics No. 2

Magnet & Camera Test Target

Seismometer

UHF Antenna (Relay)

RTG Power Source (2 Ea) (Inside Cover)

RTG Wind Cover (2 Ea)

S-Band Low Gain Antenna

Roll Engine (4 Ea)

Terminal Descent Propellant Tank (2 Ea)

Radar Altimeter Antenna & Terminal Descent Landing Radar (Underside of Lander Structure)

Leg No. 3

X-Ray Fluorescence Funnel

Terminal Descent Engine (3 Ea) 18 Nozzle Configuration

Magnets

Collector Head

Surface Sampler Boom

Biology Processor

Magnet Cleaning Brush

Leg No. 2

Landing Shock Absorber

Meteorology Boom Assembly

Meteorology Sensors

Camera (2 Ea)

GCMS Processor

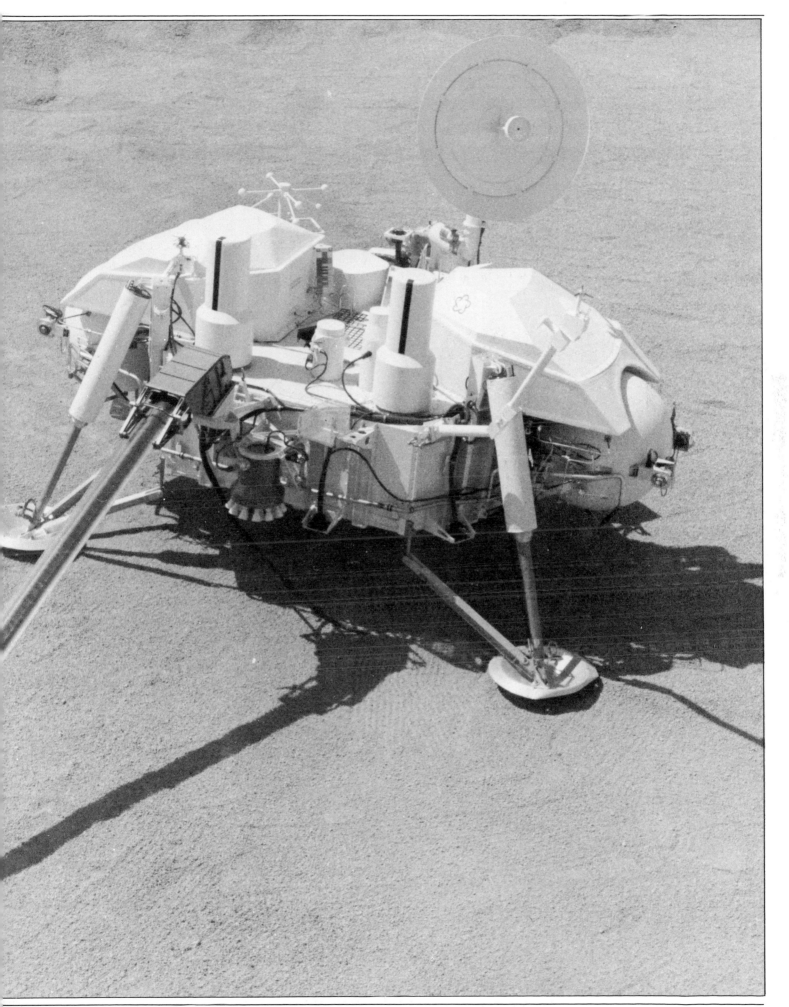

5. THE ENTERTAINER

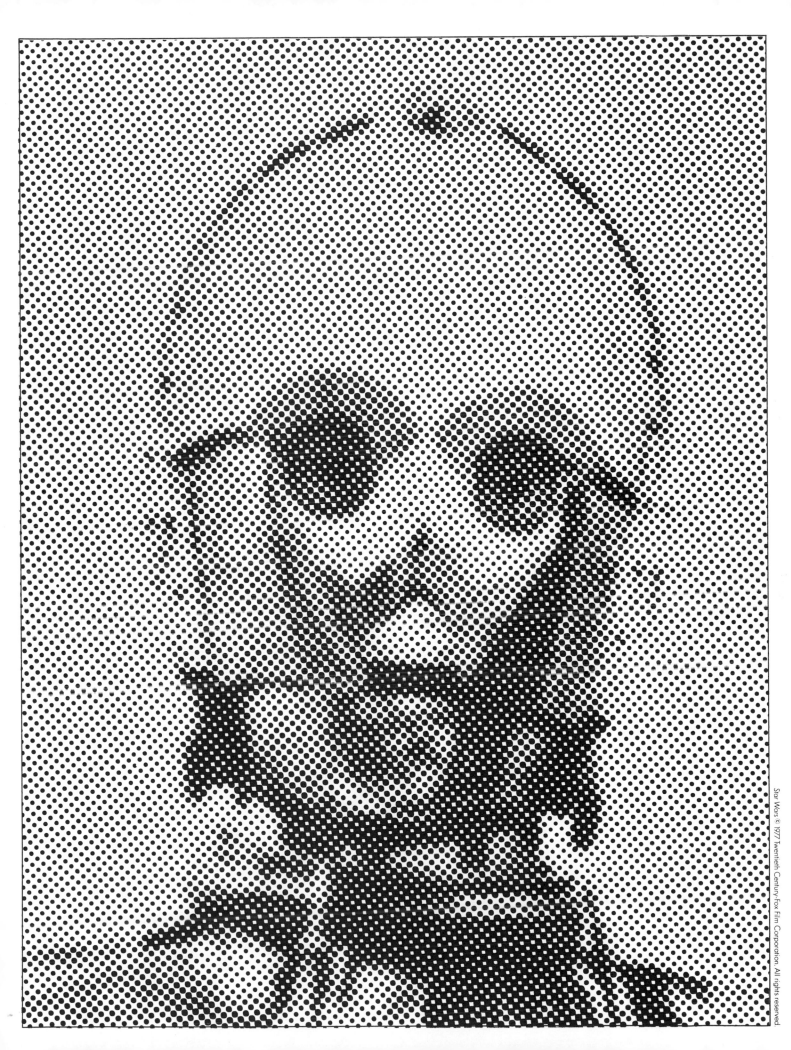

It would be a mistake to think that robots are the exclusive property of Hollywood or of science and technology. The idea of the robot is a broadly popular one, and robots often turn up in unexpected places. Constructed of tin, plastic, cardboard, or anything handy—discarded washing machine parts or odds and ends picked up from a machine shop—they are sometimes walking junk piles.

Still, they are a tribute to human ingenuity and not the product of mad scientists. They may have been whipped up for a convention, a promotional stunt, or just for the hell of it, by people who are clever with their hands. And though these robots built by amateurs may make us laugh, we are impressed by the ingenuity of the people who created them.

These robots are the real descendents of Alpha. They are the last full-scale robots that look anything like humans. They have been left behind while their smarter cousins have gone off into space or become doctors or scientists. They are the visions of yesterday, but today's playthings.

Above: In Monaco for the 1960 annual Inventors' Congress, Cosmos takes a spin down Boulevard des Moulins. Powered by an electric battery and remote-controlled, he is as elegant in his way as any strolling tourist.

Opposite, top: In 1931, when it took more than three days to cross the country by train, National Air Transport inaugurated scheduled, transcontinental service from Newark, New Jersey, to California. Westinghouse furnished a robot for the occasion. It summoned passengers to the plane, delivered a short speech, then on signal started the engines of the Ford trimotor. If the robot seems primitive by our standards, so was the flight, which took thirty-one hours.

Opposite, bottom: A woman named Sophie Ross brought this incredibly human-looking "robot" back to London with her from America in 1934. Londoners went along with the gag.

Opposite, top: Although it was invented in 1947, The English Maid has a rather Victorian solidity about her. After turning on the heater at a specified time, she boiled the water for tea and transferred it to the teapot. Then, with the heat up and breakfast ready, she rang an alarm, turned on the bedside lamp, and found a program on the radio.

Opposite, bottom: Robots are not always in good working condition. Smacking a radio or kicking a vending machine may revive them, but the most politic way of approaching a sick robot is with sympathy.

Right: The most awkward robots are often the ones with real people inside them. Tom Steele, a stunt man, inhabits this heavy and clumsy suit. He wore it as a mechanical man in a Hollywood serial made in 1953. The series sank without a trace, due perhaps to the weight of the robot. But Steele still got paid.

Far right: The evolutionary question is raised again by Anatole, a French robot made in 1955, who answered questions in the monkey house of the zoo in Rome, Italy. As a candidate for replacing man, he offered very little except strict attention to duty.

Below: This highly polished robot put together by Kleber-Colombes, a French automobile tire company, competed for attention with the Michelin man at the 1951 Paris Auto Show. A showman and a salesman, he was furnished with human features, including apple cheeks that puffed, working eyebrows, a full set of lashes, and surprisingly sad eyes.

Opposite, top: Joker's heads frequently adorned merry-go-rounds and other carnival structures produced during the last century. They were natural subjects for animation, with eyes that lighted up, mouths that opened and closed, tongues that stuck out, and other mechanical features realistic enough to scare small children.

Opposite, bottom: This toy clown graced the desk of a nineteenth-century tycoon and lighted his cigar when a button was pressed.

Top: The Ideal Toy Company had a more happy experience with Robert the Robot than occurred in *R.U.R.* The company produced half a million of these robots in the early sixties, without a hint of revolt. Robert's talking mechanism is a direct descendant of Edison's, only Robert is battery powered rather than wound with a key.

Right: The tin woodsman has been an inspiration to toy and jewelry makers ever since he was described by Frank Baum in *The Wizard of Oz.* He was one of the first robots to suffer from a rust problem. In this rendering by Joseph Leone, he stands twenty-six inches tall and is once more made of tin. His heart, however, is brass.

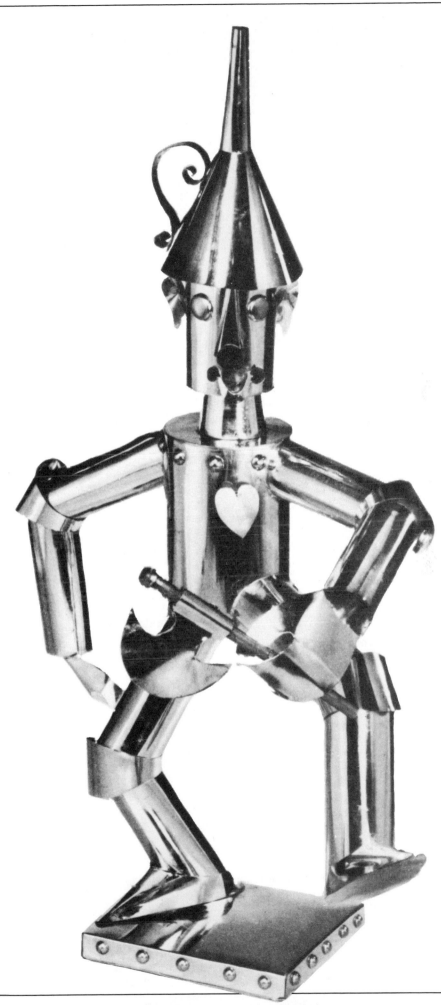

Left: Robot toys have become a booming business. This is Biotron, manufactured by Mego Corporation. He is a multi-purpose robot that can be taken apart and put together again as a space vehicle. Biotron is controlled by an astronaut who fits into a transparent control capsule on the robot's chest.

Opposite: Meet Microtron, the toy designer's ultimate solution. Microtron, has two heads, two sets of wheels and other accessories which can be combined in a variety of ways to create the toy that does everything.

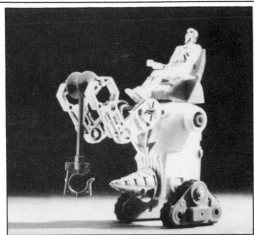

Ever since Maria appeared in Fritz Lang's 1926 film *Metropolis*, robots on the screen and on the tube have been an index of the way people feel about the technology around them. Hollywood has created clay people, statue people, metal people, nonpeople, aliens, monster creatures, androids, cyborgs, bionic look-alikes, clones—robots all, in the eyes of the script writers.

These robots may have appeared to be symbols of technology. But as often as not—when the layers of electrical makeup were peeled away—they turned out to be mere containers for old-fashioned thinking. The movies seemed to be asking: what happened to the old days when everything was simple? Whether it was Maria of *Metropolis* or HAL from *2001*, the message was that things were getting out of hand.

The message from recent films—*Star Wars*, for example—is much more reassuring. These films tell us that whatever happens in the future, human beings will always be at the center of the action, directing it. Humans may need robots, even depend on them. But humans will never be dominated by robots.

Above: *Tobor the Great* was a typical fifties robot movie. A robot-with-a-heart-of-gold story, it had Tobor (which is robot spelled backward) saving his inventors, a boy and his scientist grandfather, from evil exploiters. Tobor had an actor inside him. This did not keep him from falling over whenever a scene began to move too fast.

Left: The Golem is a statue of clay that comes alive. It is activated and controlled by a secret sign written on a piece of paper and slipped into its mouth. In this 1920 German film, which starred the great actor and director Paul Wegener, the Golem runs amok on a destructive binge before it can be stopped.

Opposite: The Colossus of New York, from the 1958 film of the same name, had a man's brain. Despite his gigantic size and fearsome look, he was capable of great humanity.

Opposite: A tough man protecting a tender woman has always been an obvious plot device. It was used in hundreds of science fiction/horror movies made during the fifties. Men seemed to like women who fainted. The robot provided a convenient opportunity.

Right: With your back against the wall, you grab any weapon that is handy. The message of man's resourcefulness often included a regression to plain old caveman violence. Here the good guys bash a robot over the head with sticks. This was usually a stop-gap measure—the hero was forced finally to use his brain to provide a happy ending.

Below: Although he did not much resemble the humans he served, Robby the Robot did have a certain air of intelligence about him, perhaps due to his egghead pate and high forehead.

From the MGM release *Forbidden Planet* © 1956 by Metro-Goldwyn-Mayer, Inc.

Opposite: *Sleeper* was full of robots. There was a dog robot, a Jewish-tailor robot, and a gay robot. Made in 1973, the film even included a chase through a robot factory. Here, Woody Allen stands in for a butler robot and is clearly bungling the job.

Above: This dramatic image from *Star Wars* shows the rich fantasy Lucas brought to his vision of future technology. He contrasts the rusty and worn with the new and shiny, the human with the alien, the rough life of the space settlers with the glazed comfort of the imperial death star. Lucas's robots are extremely functional and civilized—the only trouble with them is that they haven't been invented yet.

Right: Even a cowboy star like Gene Autry could get into trouble with robots back in the 1930's. The film was called *The Phantom Empire*. The bad guys naturally had the robots on their side.

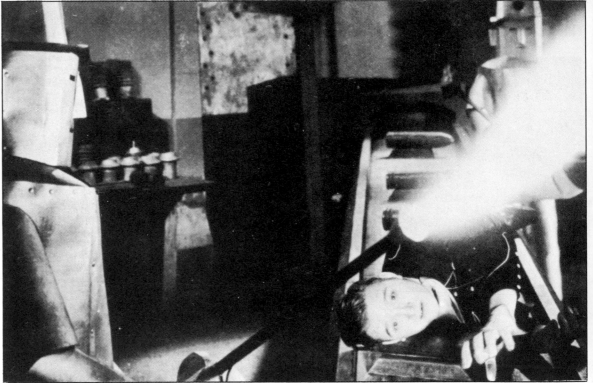

ROBOT

6. THE ART SCENE

We have always turned to our artists for a clear picture of who we really are. They have always rewarded us with something close to a collective truth. Many modern artists have used the image of the mechanical man as metaphor for living man.

The most thoroughly explored use of the robot in art is as a symbol for dehumanized humanity. Each successive school seized on it until it has become, in our time, something of a cliché. Yet we refuse to succumb to the machine. We persist with our humanity in the teeth of it.

When artists take the human form apart to explore the way it moves, the robot metaphor reappears. First, cubists, then surrealists, structuralists, and futurists all tried to fit man into the geometry of the world. Many of them found that a collection of mechanical components (the innards of the robot) worked for man as well.

Artists are still using robots as a way of measuring humans, projecting visions of the future of humanity in machine images. Sometimes the artist's vision is a warning to humanity; at other times, it is a tribute.

Right: American artists chose un-conventional subjects and ap-proached them with more than the ordinary range of techniques. This articulated catcher is as American as the game he plays.

Below: The life-size creatures Walter Einsel creates seem nor-mal and rather sedate when they are at rest. But push the plunger, turn the knob or the crank, and they go through their paces. *Man with Hat,* on the left, seems wor-ried about a stiff wind, but when you press the plunger, he lowers his hat in front of him, tries to kick it, misses, and kicks himself squarely in the face. *The Jumping Man,* next to him, does the splits like a Russian dancer while tip-ping his hat.

GROSZ, George. Republican Automatons. (1920). Watercolor, 23⅝" x 18⅝". Collection, The Museum of Modern Art, New York. Advisory Committee Fund.

Opposite: In this 1920 watercolor, George Grosz scorns empty-headed, mechanical patriotism. The flag waver represents one of the millions of maimed survivors of World War I. The man with the medal runs like clockwork.

Right: *Nude Descending a Staircase,* one of the signal works of cubism, was displayed to great clamor at the 1912 Armory Show in New York. In an attempt to represent motion on the canvas, Duchamp reduced the human body to its basic mechanics. The angles and planes that emerge are strikingly similar to our vision of a robot.

Far right: Umberto Boccioni, a futurist, saw humans as a union of the mechanistic with the organic. In *Unique Forms of Continuity in Space,* done in 1913, a humanlike figure emerges and recedes again into the metal from which he is formed. Boccioni was killed in World War I.

Below: Rube Goldberg's elaborate creations were almost all complex machines. Today we would call this a closed-loop feedback device. Goldberg simply called it *Be Your Own Dentist!*

DUCHAMP, Marcel. *Nude Descending a Staircase No. 2.*
Philadelphia Museum of Art: The Louise and Walter Arensberg Collection.

BOCCIONI, Umberto. *Unique Forms of Continuity in Space*
(1913). Bronze (small cast 1931), 43⅞ x 34⅞ x 15¾"
Collection, The Museum of Modern Art, New York. Acquired
through the Lillie P. Bliss Bequest.

Left and below: Has nature constructed human beings and animals so they function at peak efficiency? Or can nature's design be improved upon by adding new parts and "automating" them? (Consider the popularity of the Six Million Dollar Man.) In these two collages he constructed for *The New York Times* editorial pages, Jean-Claude Suarès satirizes the idea of automating either people or animals by carrying the concept to absurd lengths.

Opposite, left: Ready to take the field is Mr. Sport, a robot featured at Expo '67.

Opposite, top: The components of Paul van Hoeydonck's 1969 *CYB Head and Arm* look as if they come off the shelf in a machine shop. Although the components themselves don't actually work, they look as if they should.

Opposite, bottom: Nam June Paik, better known for his video art, is also a sculptor. This 1965 figure *Robot 456 with 20-Channel Radio Control and 10-Channel Data Recorder,* is a robot reduced to its skeletal components adorned with symbols of muscular control and response.

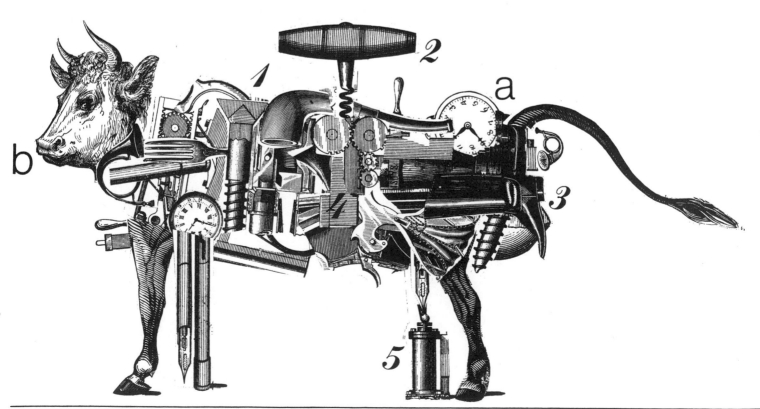

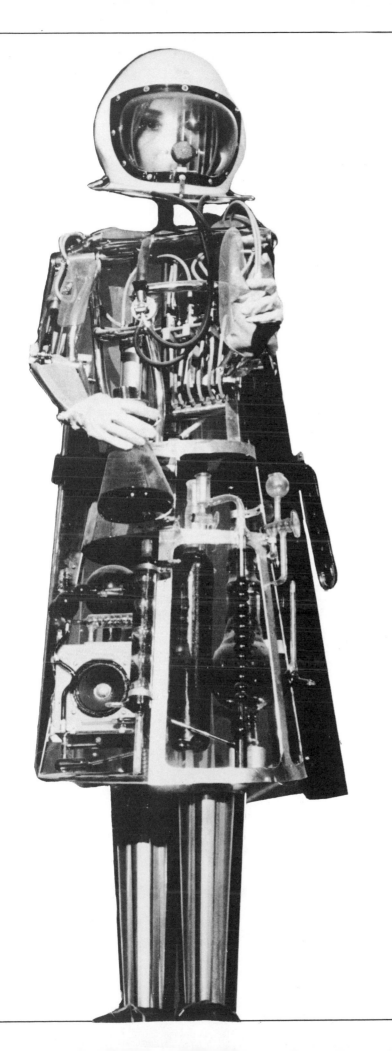

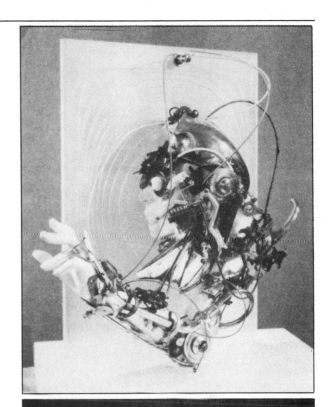

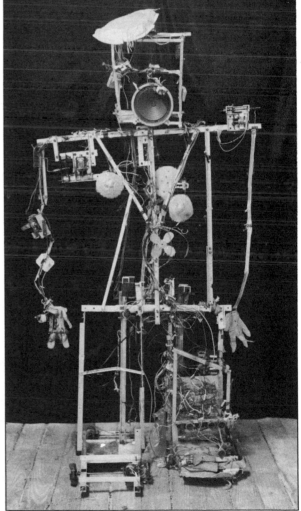

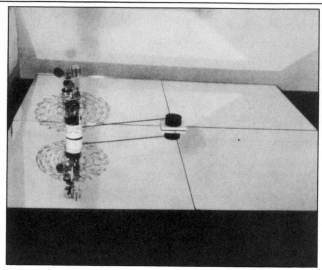

Left: James Seawright may be the first "electronic" sculptor. His pieces are unique because they not only move, make noise and glow, but they do it all according to the way the patterns of light change in the room. If there are people in the room, the shifting patterns of light become much more complex, and so do the actions of his sculpture. Seawright created *Captive* in 1966.

Opposite: *Watcher*, 1965, generated its own sound, as well as light and motion. It was the first of Seawright's creations to be able to pick up stimuli from its environment.

Below: This sculputre by Jean Tinguely, called *La Rotazaza No. 1*, does nothing useful at all. It catches balls and throws them out again, but not necessarily at whoever threw the ball. It is the mindless machine, freed from any rational guidelines.

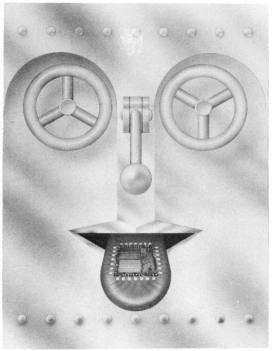

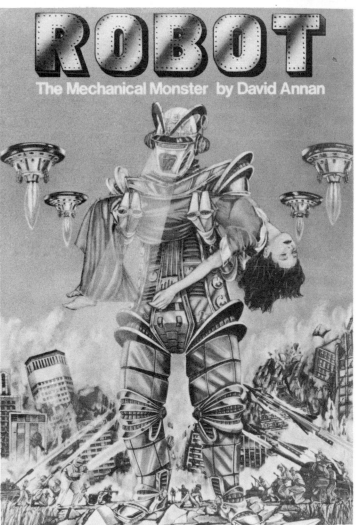

ROBOT
The Mechanical Monster by David Annan

Opposite: The expression "He has a screw loose" has long existed in American slang. In this illustration by Paul Richer for an article in *New York* magazine, Nixon is an android, bursting under the pressure of the Watergate investigation.

Above, left: Stanislaw Fernandes created this illustration for a magazine doing a cover story on automated machines. Fernandes used a robot as a symbol, working in a style similar to Leger who had created a machine world of massive dials, levers and rivets. But there is nothing archaic about the computer chip the robot holds on its tongue. The chip is the most important component that makes modern robotic devices work.

Above, right: In this 1957 *Fantastic Universe* cover, the robot becomes a Sunday painter, recording our extinct civilization. However seriously Virgil Finlay, the artist, hoped to project the future, he used images already archaic today.

Left: On the cover of a recent book, a robot snatches a girl. This is the classical monster plot used in novels from *Frankenstein* to *King Kong*. Images like this give the robot a bad name, invoking the pulp age all over again.

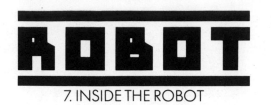

7. INSIDE THE ROBOT

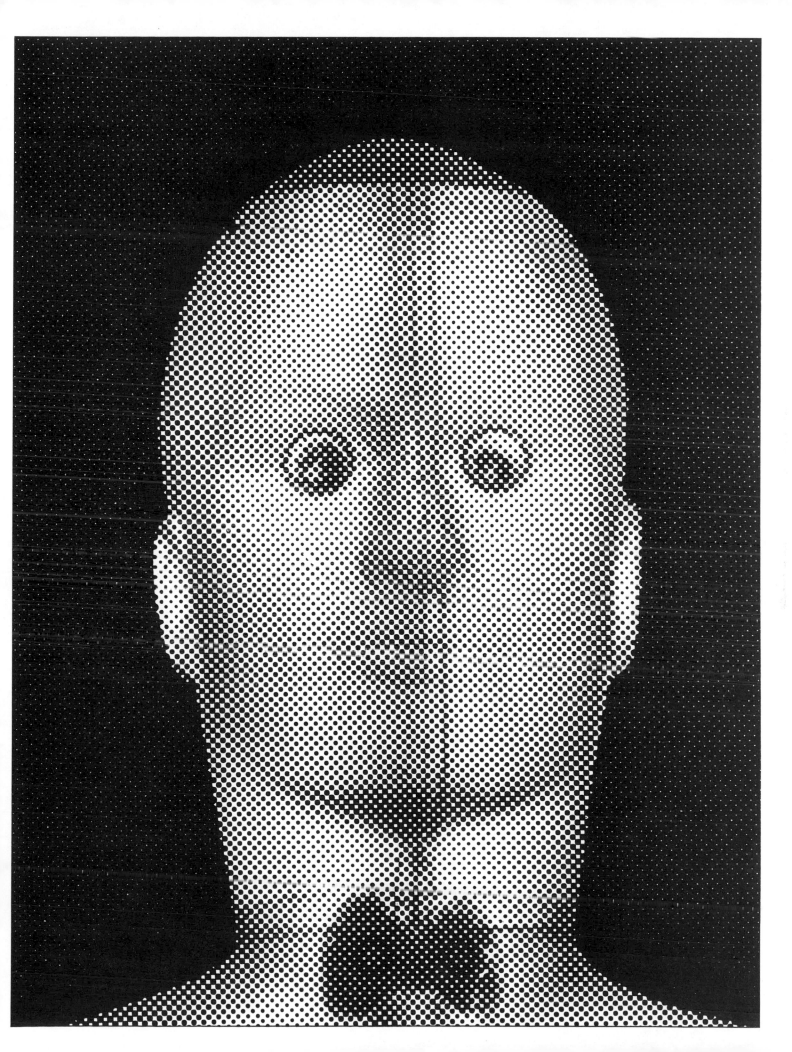

We refer to computers and other robot devices as "smart" machines. We give them tasks to do, often quite complicated ones like guiding space vehicles, performing exotic economic and scientific calculations, even planning our vacations. But as complicated as computers are, they do not really think.

They certainly *appear* to think, though. There are computers that can play chess, bridge, and other games, often beating their human opponents. Joseph Weizenvaum of MIT has even programmed a computer to imitate a psychoanalyst. There are computers that can "read" handwriting and ones that can "understand" spoken words. There are even computers that can translate from one language to another. What they do is sophisticated, but it is not thinking.

We build robots that need little or no supervision while they carry out our instructions. Many of the satellites we have sent out to space have continued to function long after their projected life was over. As independent and "clever" as these robots seem, they are not truly intelligent.

What makes these machines possible is the discovery that certain aspects of thinking can be reduced to a series of yes-no decisions, and most calculations to a series of relationships between the numbers one and zero. These calculating systems, invented by humans, bear little relation to human thought processes, but they permit machines to "think," and do it very fast.

We have only begun to penetrate the mystery of how the human brain stores and recalls data. We do not even understand clearly how the senses work, particularly sight. And the step-by-step logic the electronic brain uses does not approach the complexity (or the flexibility) of the logic used by the human brain. We are nowhere near designing a machine that approaches our own capabilities.

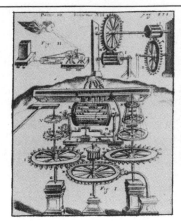

Left: This drawing by Gasper Schott dates from the seventeenth century. Although the purpose of the machine is obscure, it demonstrates the principle of programming a machine by using a perforated drum. Music boxes and player pianos use this principle.

Opposite: Two hundred years of experiments by philosophers and mathematicians culminated, finally, in Babbage's 1843 analytical machine, the ancestor of all calculators. He never completed this model, an advance over his Difference Engine. Finished, it would have included a programming device using punched cards, and a substantial memory unit consisting of 200 accumulators on twenty-five wheels.

Below: Here is a man mowing a lawn. Should we want to construct a robot mower to replace him, we would need four basic systems that correspond to human functions: (1) a sensing system for interpreting the environment, one that would tell the robot that the grass was too long, that he could rely on to help him decide the best way to do it, and that could tell him if the work was proceeding according to plan; (2) an artificial intelligence control system that would govern the robot's choices and generate its movements; (3) a system of appendages and controls that would allow the robot to manipulate the lawn mower, move it where needed; and (4) a system to power the whole thing. Analyzed from this point of view, it is amazing that all the systems a suburbanite needs to mow the lawn on Saturday afternoon are packaged so compactly in the human frame.

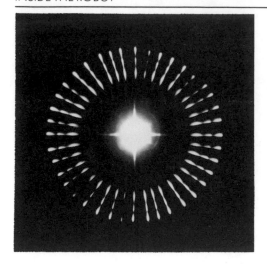

Left: Computers can now spew out answers so fast that mechanical printing systems can't keep up. Laser light, in combination with electro-photographic processes, are used for print-outs.

Below: When IBM and Dr. Howard Aiken designed this computer in 1944, it was called an Automatic Sequence Controlled Calculator. Three thousand, three hundred relays triggered mechanical devices to make it work. The whole machine weighed five tons. The next generation of computers used vacuum tubes to eliminate most of the mechanical devices, and increased the calculation speed substantially.

Opposite, top: Memory units of computers are now called cores. Each core is magnetized clockwise or counterclockwise to represent a zero or a one, a yes or a no in the system. Along with transistors, cores not only increased the speed and reliability with which a computer could function, but also reduced the size substantially, permitting today's minicomputers.

Opposite, below: A robot tool like the Technicon SMAC is really a high-speed computer with highly sophisticated hardware attached to it. SMAC is an acronym that stands for Sequential Multiple Analyzer Computer.

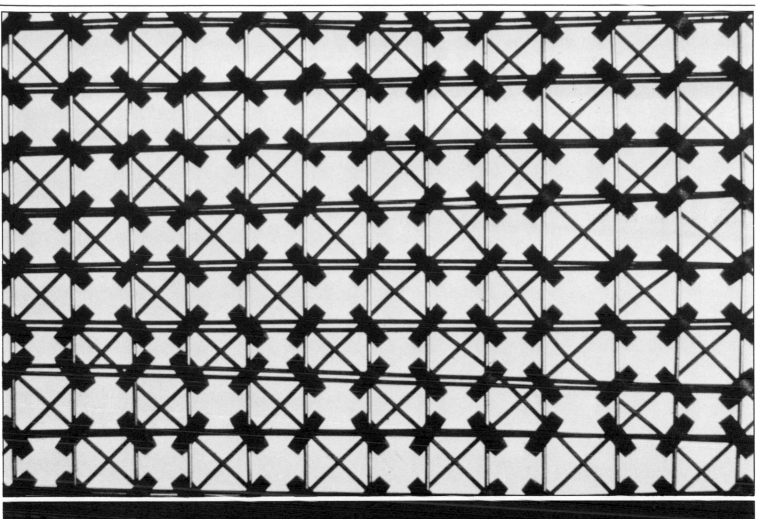

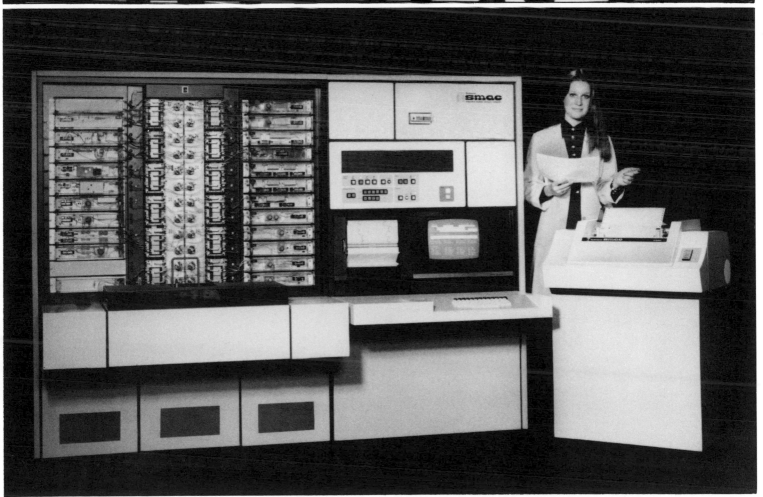

ROBOT

8. HOW TO BUILD A ROBOT

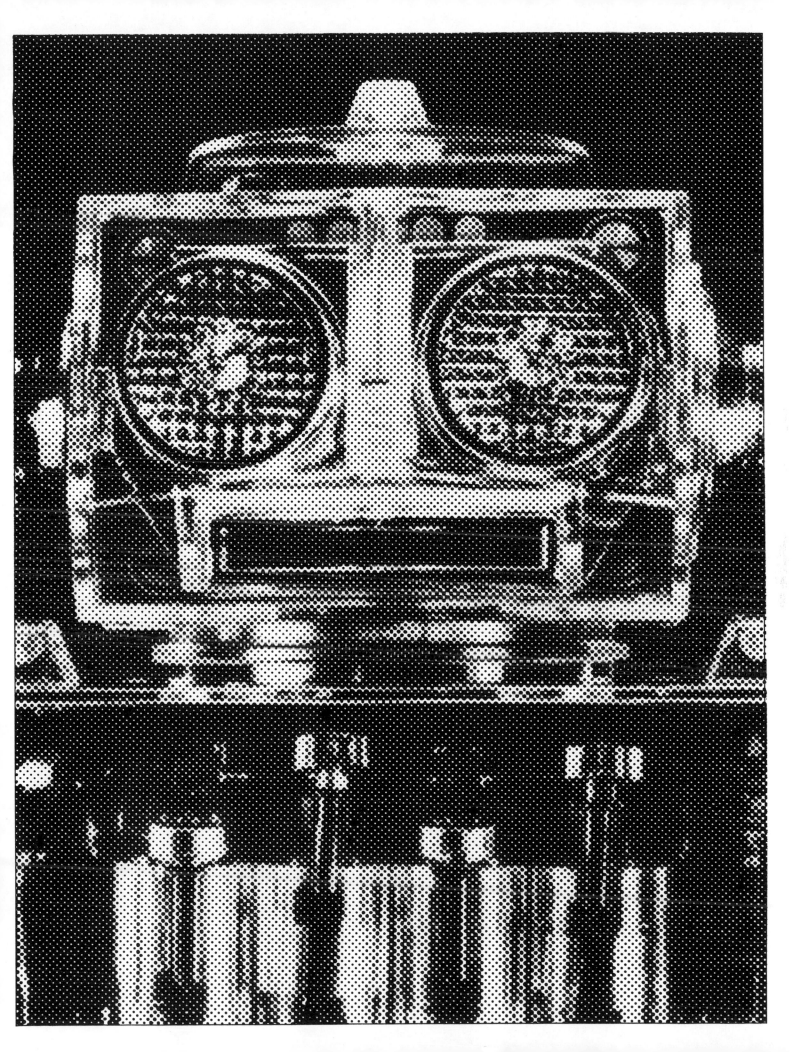

Jonathan Kaplan, a high school student in New York City, saw his first robot in a TV cartoon. The son of a civil engineer and an anthropologist, he was sure that he could make one that really worked. He added *Popular Science, Popular Electronics,* and, finally, *Scientific American* to his regular reading and produced his first functioning robot.

It was a rather crude machine, but it worked. It was followed by other creations, each one more complex and more versatile. Hours of trial and error went into the perfecting of each design. The parts he could not make himself or find on the market, he had manufactured to his specifications. (He holds U.S. Patent No. 3,997,860 for a miniature memory bit holder.)

His robots win him prizes in science fairs every year. But it is not the praise from others that motivates him and fires his interest. Out of the small closet laboratory in his bedroom have come a series of machines that point directly to the future.

Jonathan is in the process of building robot number seven. He talks with some authority about the future. He sees robots as a positive force, an extension of the natural human quest for knowledge, but not a replacement for humans. Robots may get better—may even get to be more like humans—but humans will make the choices, not machines.

Opposite: Jonathan Kaplan, ready for bed, stands behind one of his 1974 creations, a mobile platform with a mechanical arm and claw. This is the first robot Jonathan made that had a stored program. The platform can move in any of four directions, while the arm rotates, moves up and down, and the claw opens and closes. His programming device is a mechanism with prongs, powered by a slow-geared motor that activates magnetic switches.

Below: Jonathan makes some adjustments on a robot he put together for fun in 1972. Its actions are controlled by cords and pulleys.

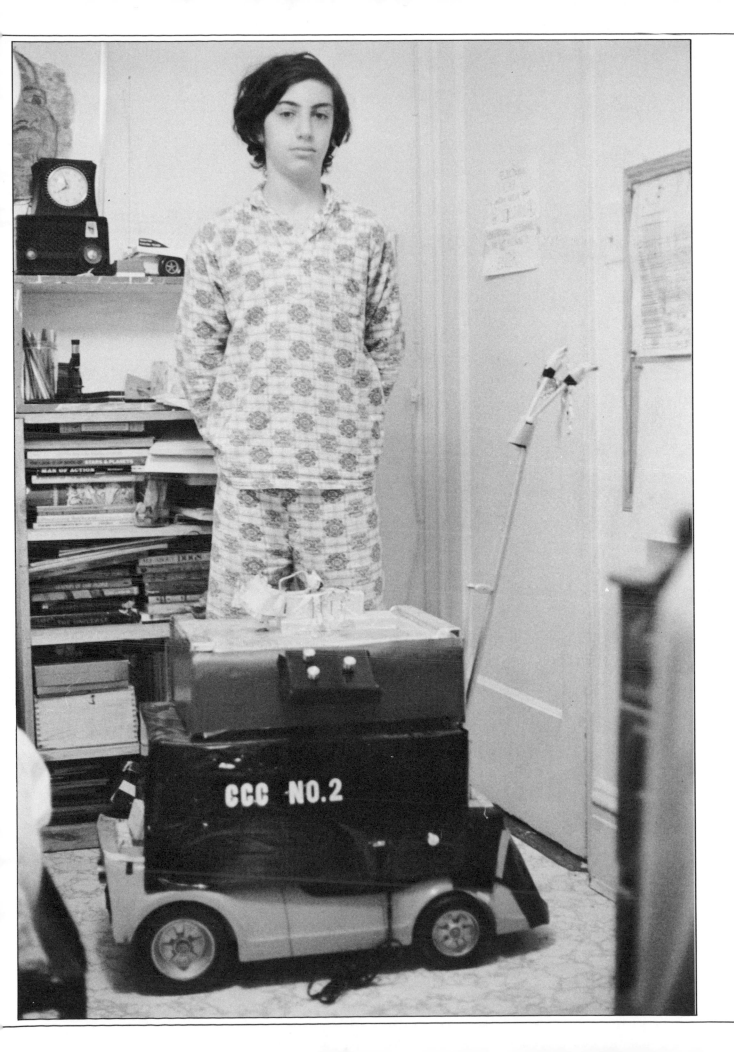

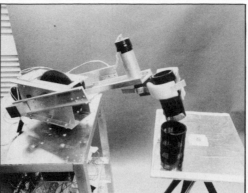

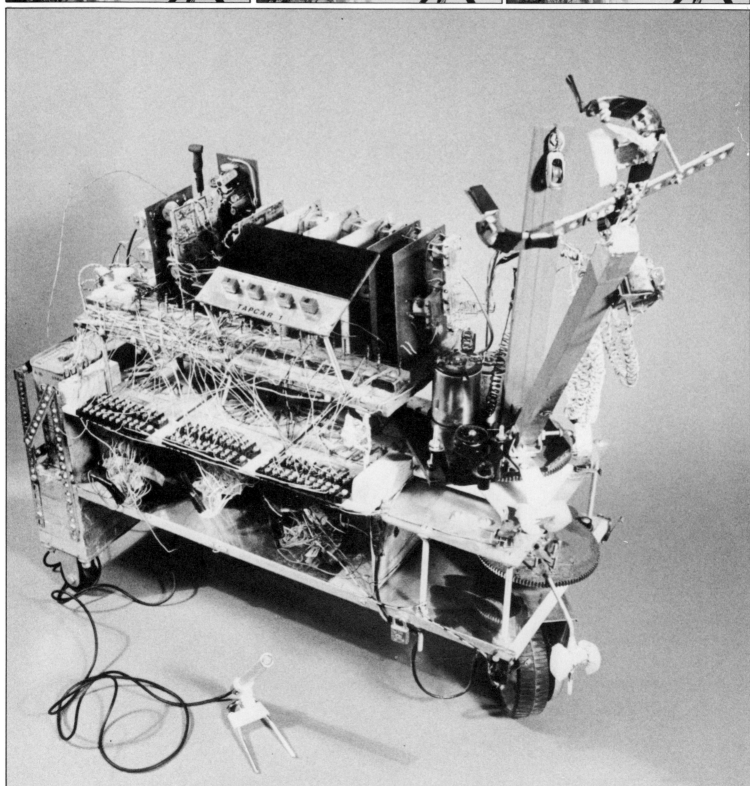

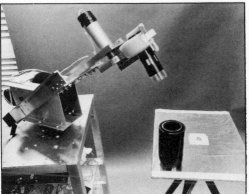

Top: This series of photographs shows Kaplan's 1977 robot deploying its arms as it picks up and sets down a series of nesting cylinders. Kaplan is now building sensing devices into the robot to provide feedback and allow it to perceive and correct its errors by itself.

Opposite: The 1976 Electronic Workman runs on rechargeable batteries. It is capable of executing three programs that have fifteen steps each. The steps are activated by a letter of the alphabet spoken at a specific pitch. The Workman can move forward and backward, left and right, can raise and lower its arm, and open and close its claw—all according to the stored programs. Each program ends by turning the Workman off and preparing it to accept the next program.

Left: Kaplan arm-wrestles with his 1977 robot. Since he made the machine and created all the circuits, he always wins.

Above: Artur Fischer developed the Fischertechnik system of interchangeable components. It is a seemingly endless assortment of mechanical, structural, and electronic modules. These can be used to create valve systems, gear systems, tools, machines, apparatus, models, and toys. In this photograph, the system has been used to create a model of an automatic package sorter. As the packages travel along the conveyor belt, the four pusher arms scan and "recognize" them, then push each package down the appropriate ramp.

Right: A Fischertechnik rendering of an automobile tire production and finishing line. The mechanisms on the left and the right transfer the tires from the central carousel to the chain-driven belt.

Left: Robots were always an ideal project to make with an Erector Set. In the past fifty years, countless children and their parents have constructed and dismantled robot figures. In an Erector Set, you could always find the right girders, wheels, gears, motors, nuts and bolts. All you had to do was supply the imagination.

Below: It would be surprising if Japan did not have its own robot man. And it does. Jiro Aizawa, a Tokyo toy researcher, made these robots between 1959 and 1963. Their names are Ichiro, Mr. Spark, Fugio, and Shinsuk. All but Shinsuk are able to walk. Japan's love for robots goes beyond toys and monsters. A substantial amount of the country's research in electronics goes into developing robots for industrial uses.

Opposite: Garco, an electronic umpire made in 1953 by the Garrett Company, was copyrighted. An offspring of aircraft technology, Garco could move his arms, hands, and face, and argue with the manager of the ball club.

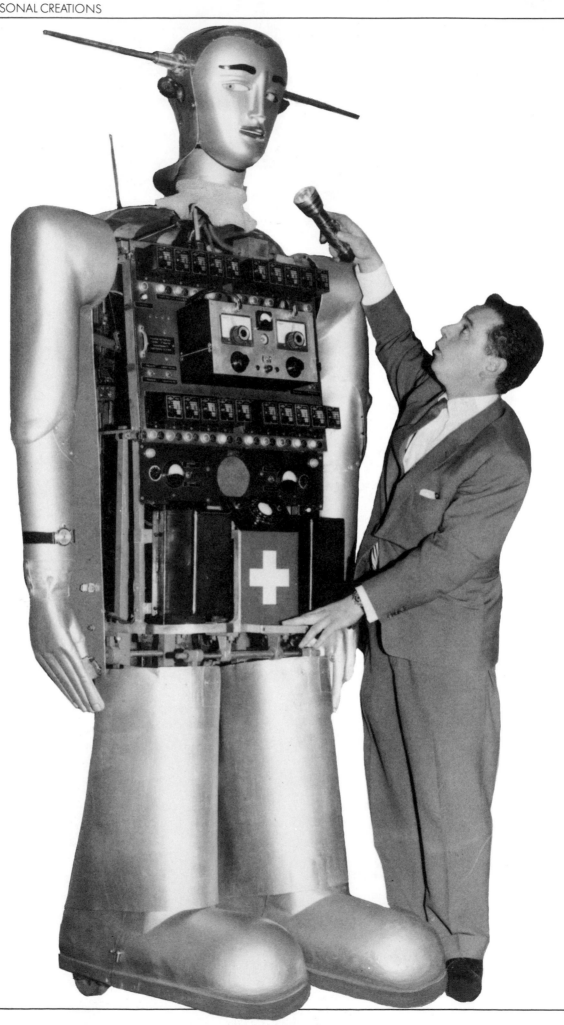

Opposite: This remote-controlled robot appeared on the scene in 1961, after ten years work by Peter Steur, a Swiss engineer. It can move its hands, walk, dance, smoke a cigarette, bow its head, and answer questions in several languages. Seen with breastplate removed, its massive inner mechanisms contrast sharply with the rather wistful expression on its face.

Above: AROK receives his instructions via an FM transmitter and receiver system that uses touch tones to call for any of thirty-six functions. Fifteen motors throughout its body are voice-activated by relays. Although it is 6′8″ and weighs 275 pounds, its center of gravity is low enough to keep it from falling over, even while lifting up to 125 pounds. Inventor Ben Skora can talk through AROK's lips and can program him to do a complete show for the entertainment of spectators.

Below: Big Looie stood 6′2″ and weighed 320 pounds. Constructed by the Rizzo brothers, John, Pat, and Steve, he retired in 1953 from Steve's electronics shop in Detroit. He was replaced by a radio-controlled aluminum man.

ROBOT

9. COPING WITH ROBOTS

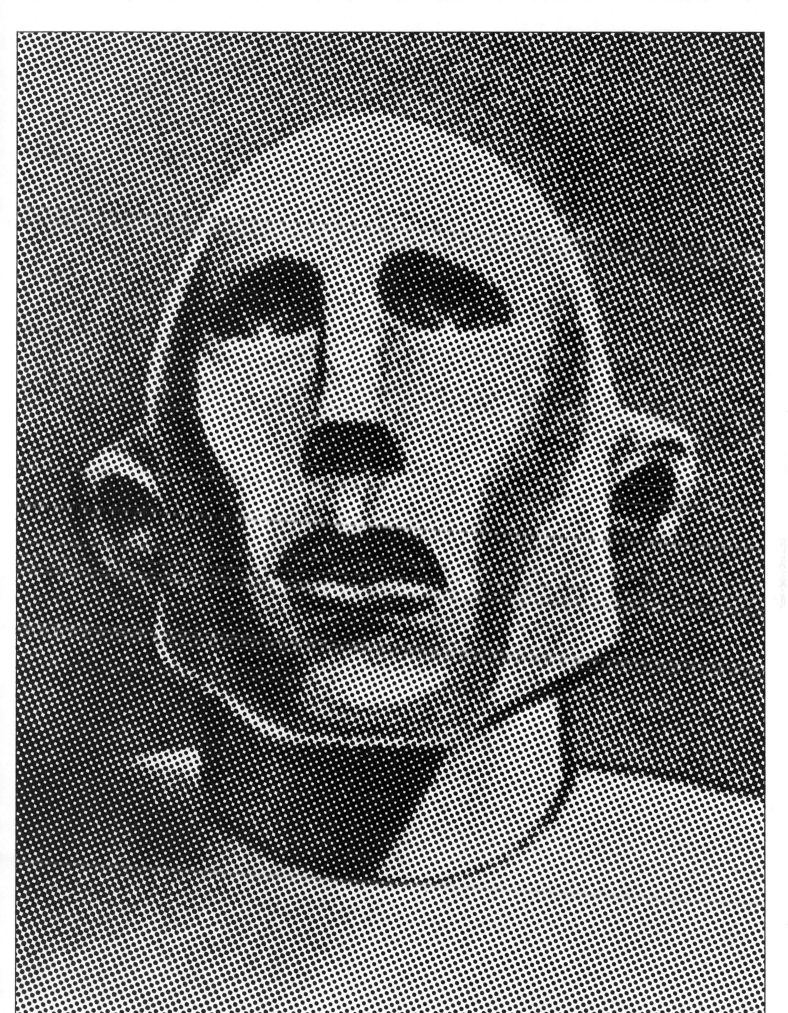

Robots are no longer visions of the future. They are here. They switch our phone calls, do our banking, maintain our supply of electric power, then bill us for these services. They wash our clothes and dishes, answer our telephones when we are not home, and take messages.

In business and industry we are even more dependent on robot devices. Automation on the assembly line has made it possible to produce new products while radically changing the cost structure. It has changed the very nature of the word work.

We use these devices, are dependent on them, but do we really trust them? A computer can get our bill wrong, then make the same computation error over and over, driving us up the wall. The arm on a robot satellite can get stuck despite "failsafe" engineering.

In some instances, we trust them with our lives. When we fly a commercial airliner, the route and other aspects of the flight have been decided by a computer. Landings in bad weather are often robot-controlled. Over 100,000 people depend on surgically implanted pacemakers to regulate their heartbeats.

It is when we trust the machine more than we trust ourselves that we get into trouble. We have to learn to acknowledge that machines are not perfect, that they are extensions of ourselves, but that they never replace our thinking or our judgment or our humanity.

The more complex the robot, the more likely it will make mistakes, break down, grow old, get dirty, get tired. We are beginning to realize that the more complicated robots become, the more their breakdowns will resemble human breakdowns.

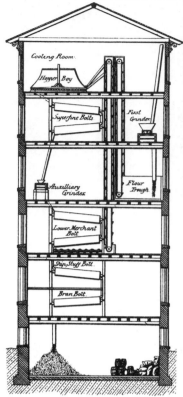

Above: Ideas for automating industry abounded in the 19th century. A patent was taken out for this automated flour-processing mill in 1849. Gravity did a lot of the work. There was not, however, a great incentive to automate, since cheap immigrant labor was pouring into the country. The idea of a machine taking away a man's job had not yet become controversial in America.

Right: These Unimate robots at work on a Fiat assembly line are a good example of the way factories are turning to robots to perform the most repetitive and boring jobs. Production lines are increasingly becoming complex machines made up of subsidiary robotic components. In turn, these supermachines are often controlled by other robotic devices.

As the industrial revolution accelerated, there were theorists who dreamed about robots that could replace workers. How wonderful, the fantasy ran, not to have to worry about human workers who got sick, argued about conditions, asked for raises, and behaved like human beings.

We now have the capability of making that dream something of a reality. Some of our industries have been almost totally automated for a century. Huge oil refineries, for example, are run by very few people. Sophisticated robotic devices bring automation to new areas of industry every day.

The other side of the coin is the workers' fear that the machine might render them obsolete. This is a problem that must be faced. Some jobs have disappeared completely from the industrial roster, and others have been changed beyond recognition. Yet, as we have seen, as more machines were introduced to industry, more employment was produced. Jobs became obsolete, but not people.

Sorting out the work that should be done by machines and the work that should be done by people is not easy. Still, we are learning more about the ways men and machines mix and the ways they do not. Machines replace men when the work is in some way "inhuman"—too repetitious, too heavy, too dangerous, too minute, too delicate.

In most cases, the robots introduced into industry have been accepted. Now that we are no longer afraid of what the machine will do to us, we are freer to choose what we want the machine to do for us. In choosing, we need to come to terms once again with what we feel makes us human. We have never before been at so decisive a turning point. The choices we make will affect us for centuries to come.

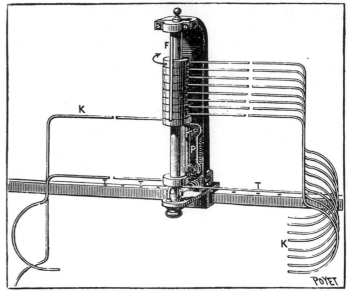

Left, above: The need for extra hands has existed ever since the first worker needed a vise. Here, a page-turner devised in 1887 by Augustin Lajarrige is contrasted with a robot manipulator by Auto Place. Robots are good at doing manipulative tasks, because they always do them exactly the same way each time.

Left, middle: Automating fire is not a new idea, as this 1893 electric match shows, but progress in this area has been noteworthy. Delostal's match used a volatile fuel on a hand-held wick, ignited by an electric spark. The Unimate welder not only provides the fire, but the hand and the series of programmed movements that allows it to weld an entire assembly without human intervention.

Left, bottom: Although the electric stenographic pen "worked," it was one of the inventions destined to die out because it was simpler to do things the old way. The Hughes Aircraft Company's automatic drafting machine, however, can be connected to a computer to produce extremely precise wiring diagrams and other complex drawings in hours. The same drawings would take days or even weeks for human draughtsmen to complete.

Working robots have not been confined just to business and industry. They have crept into our daily lives without our realizing it.

We may have dreamed of creating a single, humanoid robot capable of doing everything we ask of it. But what we've done in practice is invent simpler robots to do specific jobs. We call them by names related to the tasks they perform—refrigerators, washing machines, pocket calculators, automatic timers. We do not actually think of them as robots at all.

To a great extent we have become dependent on these specialized robots. When we are subjected to blackouts, for example, or other mechanical breakdowns, we become aware how much we expect systems to function smoothly and automatically. If we plan in the future to bring more complicated systems into our lives, they must be at least as efficient and trouble-free as the ones we already have.

The development of the microcomputer will result in a wave of new robotic devices that will affect our lives. We can already buy games and toys that make use of a computer chip (the game board is our television screen). When we have microcomputers in our homes or carry them in our pockets, we will be able to create another generation of complex machines to serve us.

But no matter how complicated they become, they will not be thinking machines. Whether they play games with us, make us laugh, or perform our work, we are still the boss.

Opposite: Goro, a Japanese robot, takes a stroll through a school playground. Children often seem to relate easily to robots, regarding them as just another big toy or even a playmate. Robots are hardly ideal companions, but they have been programmed to play chess, poker and bridge, although without using an actual deck of cards. Other games, like Pong, involving robot adversaries, can be played on the screen of an ordinary television set. As robotic devices become more familar to us, we may ask them to fill more of our leisure time.

Right: AROK takes inventor Ben Skora's dog, Benji, for a walk. In addition to walking the dog, AROK takes out the garbage and performs other household chores, after a fashion. The multi-purpose domestic robot of the future would probably be less humanoid and more functional. The more precisely an activity can be defined (or grouped with other related activities) the easier it is to invent a robot to perform it.

10. THE FUTURE

It's entirely possible that in the future we will be able to stuff so many different programs into our robots that their capabilities will appear to rival our own. And since we can retrieve stored data and beam it anywhere in the world in a split second, robots may not even need to carry around most of their "brains." We can set up a central bank with programs for every imaginable task.

You will probably be able to rent robots. You might order a compact model for personal use, and a larger, more powerful one for complex calculations or heavier work, or even a mammoth one, capable of intricate sensory perceptions, able to perform several related tasks at the same time. The robot will get its instructions, do as it is told, and report the results.

Such a robot may become a universal tool, using plug-in devices that computer people call terminals and interfaces. You might, for example, plug the robot into your car and punch out a destination, and it will drive you there. It would certainly cut your lawn, if asked. Or more important, if you're a farmer, it might stand ready to plow your fields and plant your corn crop.

In factories, robots might be programmed with all the necessary instructions to make a product. A supervisory computer might then dispatch robots from one part of the factory to another as they are needed to maintain the production flow. Robots might automatically plug themselves in and out of the assembly line. Factories would then need no shifts. There would be no halt in production, except for breakdowns and maintenance.

It seems inevitable that robots and robot devices will make enormous contributions to the productivity of our society, while concurrently increasing our leisure time. What we do with that time—whether we make it productive in terms of our humanity—will determine the future relationship of man to machine.

Above: The finger on the button. Within a few generations we have gone from the age of steel to the machine age and beyond. In today's complex world, when we press the button, we set in motion entire sets of actions that produce consequences we are only dimly aware of. Between the button and the result are machines and systems—hidden under the skin, behind the wall, out of sight—that are as mysterious to us as the surface of the moon. If we are to control our world, we have to become more aware of what goes on behind that button.

Right: We can now instruct a computer to design and build a new computer. The new computer may then make its "creator" obsolete. In the quest for additional capability and speed, many unusual approaches have been tried in designing computers. This is a logic system that uses fluid circuits. Here, the working fluid is air (indicated by the white areas).

If robots and robot devices do indeed perform a great deal of our work in the future, will we have achieved the dream of Aristotle? Over 2,000 years ago, he wrote: "If every instrument could accomplish its own work, obeying or anticipating the will of others...if the shuttle could weave, and the pick touch the lyre, without a hand to guide them, chief workmen would not need servants, nor masters slaves."

Will this be the future?

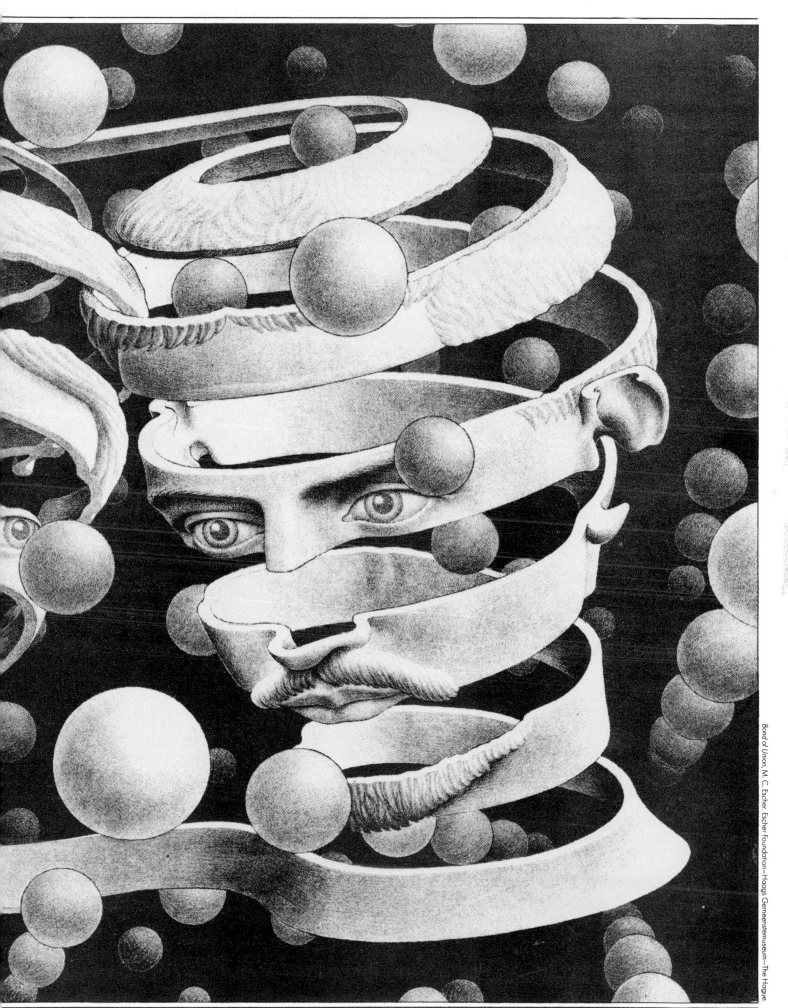

GLOSSARY

Android: Science fiction term used to describe an automaton or robot.

Anthropoid: Resembling a human form.

Artificial intelligence: Substitute for the functions of the human brain.

Automation: Science and technology that deals with theory and construction of self-controlled machines and systems.

Automaton: Machine, often in human form, incorporating mechanisms that perform without human intervention.

Biofeedback: Biological actions that operate in response to signals registering on an input mechanism.

Bionics: Science of relating biological processes to engineering and systems problems.

Clone: Creature or plant descended from a single individual without recourse to the normal reproductive process.

Closed loop: Sequential series of actions performed by a machine.

Cognition: Faculty of knowing.

Cybernetics: Science of control, as related to the structure and function of the human brain.

Cyborg: In fiction, an artificially produced human being.

Drone: Mechanism that can operate without direct human guidance.

Enhancement: Increased functional utility of human beings through mechanical/electronic means.

Exoskeleton: External supporting structure of an animal or mechanical system.

Feedback: Process in which the factors that produce a result are themselves modified by that result.

Genetic engineering: Artificial manipulation of gene structure.

Governor: Device that regulates the speed, output, or motion of a mechanism.

Humanoid: Early ancestor of *Homo sapiens.* In science fiction, an intelligent alien creature.

Industrial robot: Robot that performs specific work tasks such as welding or handling of goods and materials.

Logic: Science of reasoning and calculating correctly.

Manipulator: Mechanical appendage that works or operates remotely.

Memory storage: Various processes and mechanisms, such as magnetic cores, used in computers to store programs and data.

Open loop: Controlled action of a mechanism through feedback.

Programming: Sequencing of operations by input of coded data for processing by a computer.

Robot: Machine that simulates the function or appearance of a human being.

Robot generation: Level of development in robot design and engineering.

Simulation: Having the appearance of a condition, environment, creature, or function.

Solid state: Technology based on the use of conducting materials to modify electronic signals.

System: Combination of parts or organs arranged to perform a unified function.

Technology: Science or terminology of a particular industrial art.

Transistor: Solid state electronic device, not requiring a vacuum to operate.

BIBLIOGRAPHY

Agel, Jerome, editor. *The Making of Kubrick's 2001.* New York, New American Library, 1970. Documentation of the techniques used in creating this science fiction classic.

Annan, David. *Robot, The Mechanical Monster.* London, Bounty Books, 1976. Robots as science fiction monsters.

Asimov, Isaac. *I, Robot.,* New York, Doubleday, 1950. Highly original science fiction stories concerning the development and social consequences of robots.

Binder, Eando. *Adam Link, Robot.* New York, Paperback Library, 1965. The early Binder robot as fictional hero.

Burnham, Jack. *Beyond Modern Sculpture.* New York, George Braziller, 1968. An examination of the trends of modern sculpture, including cybernetic sculpture.

Capek, Karel. *R.U.R.* London, Oxford University Press, 1961. The play that coined the word robot and set the stage for robots as machines that threatened humanity.

Chapuis, Alfred, and Droz, Edmund. *Les Automates.* Neuchâtel, Switzerland, 1949. The primary history of automatons.

Clarens, Carlos. *Horror Film.* New York, Putnam's, 1967. History of horror films with special attention given to Fritz Lang.

Clarke, Arthur C. *Profiles of the Future.* New York, Harper & Row, 1968. Clarke's daring vision of the world of tomorrow.

Davis, Douglas. *Art and the Future.* New York, Praeger, 1973. Comprehensive examination of the history of art as influenced by technology.

Eco, Umberto, and Zorzoli, G.B., *The Picture History of Inventions.* New York, Macmillan, 1963. Intelligent history of mechanical inventions.

Florescu, Radu. *In Search of Frankenstein.* New York, Warner, 1975. An engrossing documentation of the Frankenstein story, tracing the idea of artificial life.

Frewin, Antony. *One Hundred Years of Science-Fiction Illustration.* New York, Pyramid, 1975. Survey of nineteenth-century and early twentieth-century science fiction illustration, intelligently documented.

George, Frank, and Humphries, John. *The Robots Are Coming.* Manchester, England, NCC Publications, 1974. A review of the contemporary technical state of the art of robots.

Gunn, James. *Alternate Worlds.* Englewood Cliffs, N.J., Prentice-Hall, 1975. An enlightening history of science fiction.

Kelly, Lloyd L. *The Pilot Maker.* New York, Grosset & Dunlap, 1970. All about aircraft simulation.

Kyle, David. *A Pictorial History of Science Fiction.* London, Hamlyn, 1976. History of ideas of films, pulps, novels and illustrations in science fiction to the mid-1970s.

Lewis, Arthur O., editor. *Of Men and Machines.* New York, Dutton, 1968. Essays on the relationship between humans and technology.

Marx, Leo. *The Machine in the Garden.* London, Oxford University Press, 1964. Essays on the advent of machines on the American landscape.

McHale, John. *The Future of the Future.* New York, Ballantine, 1967. Predictions of future technological developments.

Mumford, Lewis. *Technics and Civilization.* New York, Harbinger, 1963. A philosophical review of the development of modern technology.

Pekelis, Victor. *Cybernetics A to Z.* Moscow, Mir Publishers, 1970. A technical but readable treatise on cybernetics and computer ideas.

Singer, Holmyard; Hall, and Williams. *A History of Technology.* London, Oxford University Press, 1957. Comprehensive overview of the world's technical and mechanical history.

Singh, Jagjit. *Great Ideas in Information Theory, Language, and Cybernetics.* New York, Dover, 1966. Technical studies of information theory.

Toffler, Alvin. *Future Shock.* New York, Random House, 1970. Journalistic look at the potential, good and bad, of the future.

Walter, W. Grey. *The Living Brain.* New York, Norton, 1953. A research pioneer looks at the brain in relation to modern science.

ACKNOWLEDGEMENTS continued from copyright page.

Grateful acknowledgement is made to the following parties who have given permission for the reproduction of copyright works. Without their cooperation the value of this book would have been greatly diminished. If there are omissions or discrepancies, please contact the editors; amends will be made in future editions.

Amazing Stories: Copyright 1928 by Experimenter Publishing Co. with arrangement with Ultimate Publishing Co., Inc.:57, 60T

Analog: Copyright © 1972 by The Conde Nast Publications Inc. Used with permission of Frank Kelly Freas:66T

Argosy All-Story Weekly:56T

Isaac Asimov: From *I, Robot* by Isaac Asimov. Copyright © by Isaac Asimov. Used by permission of Doubleday & Company, Inc.:63T

Astounding Stories: Copyright © 1953 by Street & Smith Publications Inc. Used with permission of Frank Kelly Freas:145

Copyright © 1934 by Street & Smith Publications Inc. Copyright © 1962 [renewed] by The Conde Nast Publications Inc.:13TR

Auto Place Incorporated:76–77, 149T

Baxter Travenol Laboratories, Inc.:88T

Brookhaven National Laboratories:127

Buck Rogers in the 25th Century® used with permission of Robert C. Dille, Carmel, Ca. 93923:58T

Casa editrice.From *History of Inventions* by Umberto Eco and G. B. Zorzoli, published by Casa editrice Valentino Bompiani & Co.:128T, 129

Cinemabilia:112B

Herman Cohen Productions, Inc.: *Target Earth*: 110–111

Ron Dilg:84

Phillippe Druillet and *Heavy Metal*:67

Dunlap and Associates, Inc.:89

Walter Einsel:115, 116, 117

Ed Emshwiller "Emsh". Used with permission of *Galaxy* Magazine: Universal Publishing and Distributing Corporation.:62T, 63B

Fantastic Universe:125TR

Fantasy:59

Stanislaw Fernandes for *Business Week*:125TL

fischertechnik: Fischer-Werke, Artur Fischer GmbH & Co.:138T, 138–139

Courtesy of Franklin Institute:16

Future Science Fiction:55

General Electric Company, Research and Development Center:74, 75, 79B

German National Tourist Office: 33

Bob Giusti and Balantine Books, from the cover of *Who*:153

Rube Goldberg © King Features Syndicate 1977. World Rights Reserved:119B

Dr. Ralph Goldman, U. S. Army Research Institute of Environmental Medicine:85

Hart Publishing: From *Catalog of the Unusual* by Harold H. Hart. Copyright © 1973 by Hart Publishing Company, Inc.:105R

© 1967 Christian Herdeg:121 L

Hoy:61

Hughes Aircraft Company:21, 71, 80–81, 81 T, 149B

IBM Corporation:130, 131 T, 154, 155

© Ideal Toy Corporation:105L

IIT Research Institute:79T

The Illustrated London News:9, 17, 37B, 39B

Italian Government Travel Office:32

Courtesy of Janus Films:12B, 15, 18L, 48–49

Professor Flora S. Kaplan:134, 135

Kronen Gallery:117T

Lear Siegler Corporation:20B

Lorimer Publishing: From *Robot: The Mechanical Monster* by David Annan, published by Lorimer Publishing Ltd.:125B

Lynx:65

Martin Marietta Corporation: 13B, 96T, 96–97

Medtronic:86T

© 1977 Mego Corp.:106, 107

© 1965 by Peter Moore:121 B

André Morain:122B

© 1967 Gray Morrow. Used with permission of *Galaxy* Magazine: Universal Publishing and Distributing Corporation :64

NASA:18R, 92–93, 94–95, 96B

National Institutes of Health:90

The New York Public Library: Picture Collection:36, 44B

Theatre Collection: The New York Public Library at Lincoln Center; Astor, Lenox and Tilden Foundations:46–47

The New York Times:101 T

Richard Pan:3, 4, 5, 6, 69, 133, 136, 137

© 1958 Paramount Pictures Corporation. All rights reserved.:109

Philosophical Library: Plate 53 from T. E. Ivall's *Electronic Computers*. Permission granted by Philosophical Library, Inc.:70T

Programmed and Remote Systems Corp.:81 B

Queens Devices, Inc.:70B

From *Tobor the Great*: Republic Pictures.:108T

Paul Richer:124

Scoops:58B

James Seawright:122T, 123

Singer Aerospace and Marine Systems:82–83, 83T

Ben Skora:143T, 151

J.-C. Suarès:120

Technicon Instruments Corporation:87, 131 B

Texas Heart Institute, Houston, Texas:91

Unimation, Inc.:72–73, 78, 146–147, 149C

Paul van Hoeydonck:121 T

Veterans' Administration:88B

Weird Tales:56B

Wide World Photos:19R, 50, 51, 100, 101 B, 102, 103, 140, 141, 142, 143B, 150